FCAnaes PART 1 PRACTICE EXAMS

Wynne Aveling MA MB BChir FCAnaes
Consultant Anaesthetist

Stuart Ingram MBBS FCAnaes
Consultant Anaesthetist

Lesley Bromley BSc MBBS FCAnaes
Senior Lecturer in Anaesthetics

The University College and Middlesex Hospitals

PASTEST
KNUTSFORD
CHESHIRE

© 1986 and 1991 PASTEST
Rankin House
Parkgate Estate
Knutsford
Cheshire WA16 8DX
Tel: 0565 755226

First published 1986
Reprinted 1988
Second edition 1991
Reprinted 1992

A catalogue record for this book is available from the British Library.

ISBN 0–906896–71–1

Text prepared by Turner Associates, Knutsford, Cheshire.
Phototypeset by Speedset Ltd, Ellesmere Port.
Printed by Staples Ltd, Rochester, Kent.

CONTENTS

PREFACE

When the moment finally comes and the numbers are called out, some will step forward to hear that they have passed. They will head for the pub to enjoy the well earned glow of self confidence that is induced by a gin and tonic, rejoicing in the knowledge that one exam at least, is now safely behind them. But at the other end of the bar there will gather others whose numbers were not called, in all probability they will have worked and studied just as hard and may well know just as much, but as they stare balefully into their mug of bitter they know that they will be back again in a few months for another go.

What made the difference? Some will say luck, or perhaps it was the misfortune of encountering for the orals one of those examiners so notorious, that in the waiting room their name is not even mentioned in hushed whispers. The real answer is probably much simpler and can be summarised as "organisation and presentation", otherwise referred to as examination technique. The candidate who passed appreciated that the exam is not just about what you have learnt but it is about the ability to recall and relay what you have learnt.

The object of this book is to help those preparing for the exam to achieve that ability and thus to ensure that the publicans sell rather more gin and tonic and rather less bitter.

The idea of writing this book came from our association with others, in setting up and running the North London Course for the Part 1 exam. This course started in the autumn of 1984 and we believe that it has shown that although one of the original intentions of changing the format of the FCAnaesthetists Part 1 examination was to encourage teaching by Consultants of the SHOs in their own hospitals, this often needs to be supplemented. In addition it is vital to know exactly how the exam is being conducted and to talk at length with candidates both successful and unsuccessful to learn how teaching should be modified to improve the chances of success. We are grateful to many students on the North London Course who have helped with this feedback and have acted as guinea pigs in the selection of much of the material included here. We would also wish to acknowledge the help of our many clinical colleagues who have provided material for inclusion in this book.

Consultants can sit in at the orals and see both the way in which questions are being asked and also where the candidates show weaknesses in answering. You should urge any Consultant interested in teaching to take up this opportunity to sit in. The College of Anaesthetists publishes a "Guide to Training" (May 1990) which gives information about the format of their exams together with other useful information on anaesthetic training. It is essential to obtain a copy. We have quoted where relevant from this booklet and in general this information has been placed between quotation marks.

HOW TO USE THIS BOOK

There are sections to help with each aspect of the exam, providing general advice on examination technique, as well as specific questions carefully structured to test your ability and to help you to appreciate the standard required. To gain full benefit from what is provided here, you will need the help of a more senior anaesthetist to advise you on the quality of your written answers and the co-operation of a colleague who is also studying for the exam or who has recently taken it, to enable the material provided in relation to the clinical oral, to be used to create the situation of a 'Mock Viva'.

The answer sections have all been gathered at the end of the book, to try to discourage any tendency read the answers before the questions!

THE FCAnaes PART 1 EXAMINATION

There are four sections:

1. 60 multiple choice questions – 2 hours
2. 7 compulsory written answers – 3 hours
3. Clinical oral with two examiners using guided questions – 25 minutes. This is preceded by a ten-minute period during which candidates study some written information concerning a hypothetical patient together with the results of relevant investigations. There are also other clinical problems related to visual material such as X-rays, ECGs, biochemical or haematological results. All candidates who are simultaneously examined will receive the same material and broadly similar questioning.
4. Oral with two examiners, approximately half of which is devoted to the physical principles underlying the working and safe use of commonly used anaesthetic and monitoring apparatus – 30 minutes.

STANDARD REQUIRED

The Part 1 is intended to be taken towards the end of the first year of anaesthesia, although there is no specific requirement to have worked for a set time before sitting the exam, it "tests, the fundamentals of clinical practice, the knowledge needed to practise independently for most types of routine and some emergency anaesthesia."

In order to pass, you should give the correct answers and give them with some confidence and promptness. You need to demonstrate good judgement by dealing with real problems rather than getting bogged down with some perceived theoretical difficulty. When presented with questions, especially in the orals, that relate to clinical situations you should always adopt a cautious approach based upon the principles described in the standard anaesthetic textbooks. It is essential to show that you are a sensible and above all a safe anaesthetist.

SYLLABUS

"Although no syllabus is issued for any part of the examination, the following outline covers the main areas of knowledge and experience with which you will be expected to be familiar.

A. Goals of the examination

1. To demonstrate knowledge of how to administer a general or local anaesthetic to a fit adult patient for a straightforward elective in-patient or out-patient surgical procedure and to provide appropriate postoperative pain relief.

2. To demonstrate knowledge of the principles of care of children (excluding neonates) undergoing anaesthesia for straightforward surgical procedures including ENT, eye and dental surgery.

3. To demonstrate knowledge of immediate care and resuscitation in patients of all ages to the level of advanced cardio-pulmonary resuscitation (CPR).

4. To demonstrate knowledge required to deal with emergencies before, during and after anaesthesia, and the ability to stabilise a patient's condition until senior assistance can be obtained.

5. To demonstrate a knowledge of the principles of obstetric analgesia and anaesthesia.

B. Main areas covered in the examination

1. Commonly used anaesthetic equipment and techniques
Physical principles underlying the function of anaesthetic machines and delivery systems. Methods of checking their performance in clinical practice. Related anaesthetic equipment, together with equipment used for local anaesthesia and resuscitation. Complications occurring during anaesthesia and the recovery period. Basic techniques for administering general anaesthesia. The principles of patient monitoring of anaesthetised and unconscious patients, and the recording of relevant data. Accuracy and limitations of patient monitoring equipment.

2. Pre-operative Assessment
Preoperative assessment of a patient of any age (excluding neonates) for elective or emergency surgery including relevant investigations. Preparation of patients for anaesthesia, including fluid administration. Understanding of the commoner medical diseases and surgical disorders and their implications for anaesthesia. Ability to discern when more senior anaesthetic help will be required.

3. Applied basic sciences
Knowledge of the relevant anatomy, physiology and pharmacology to allow an effective choice of technique for the patients listed under A above, including:
    (i) Anatomical knowledge relevant to general anaesthesia, including knowledge of upper limb, intercostal and field blocks and the principles of spinal and epidural techniques with their complications.

(ii) Basic physiological principles together with an understanding of the physiological effects of commonly used anaesthetic agents and techniques.

(iii) The pharmacology of drugs commonly encountered in anaesthetic practice, together with their dosage, side effects and interactions with other drugs.

4. Care of the patient recovering from anaesthesia and of the unconscious patient in the accident and emergency department or other environment.

5. Resuscitation of patients with airway problems, ventilation problems, hypovolaemia, circulatory failure or cardiac arrest."

The level of knowledge required in basic sciences at Part 1 often causes surprise to candidates who imagine that this is the purpose of the Part 2. It is not sufficient to rely on what can be recollected from pre-clinical examinations; physiology, pharmacology and anatomy, as applied to anaesthesia, need to be systematically revised.

It may well be that many candidates will not have had direct involvement with some of the types of surgery that are specified and it is important to identify any deficiencies in one's experience and to be sure that these topics are covered in preparing for the exam. Obstetrics and anaesthesia for children are not usually regarded as being within the competence of a first year SHO, but they are included in the syllabus and to pass, it is necessary to be able to show an awareness of the potential problems in these areas as well as a knowledge of how they should be managed. The inclusion of commonly used regional anaesthetic techniques in the syllabus is often not appreciated by candidates who have failed to prepare for the questions that are asked.

MARKING SYSTEM
"The College uses a 4-point close marking system in all its examinations, the marks used being:

2+   Good pass
2   Pass
1+   Fail by a small margin
1   Bad fail

The following marks are required to pass in Part 1:
2,2,2,1+ or better."

3

In all parts of the examination the performance of borderline candidates is reviewed by all the examiners before the final marks are awarded.

It can be seen that with this marking system it not possible to pass if marked 1 on any part and even a single 1+ can be very difficult to recover from, therefore to pass, candidates should try to achieve a good average standard in all the parts of the examination, and not patches of brilliance alternating with disaster.

MCQs are marked by computer and all other elements are marked by pairs of examiners working independently. No pair of examiners marks more than one element for any individual candidate, nor are they aware of the marks awarded by any other pairs of examiners for any candidate until that candidate's examination is completed.

THE MULTIPLE CHOICE QUESTION PAPER

The use of MCQ papers is now so widespread in medical examinations that anyone sitting the FCAnaes Part 1 will without doubt have met them before, but it is important to remember their advantages and disadvantages. Unlike essays and orals which tend to be subjective, MCQs enable an objective test of factual knowledge to be made over a wide area of the syllabus. They can however be criticised for being a superficial test, for they do not assess the ability to weigh up the relative importance of information as may be required in clinical situations.

In some subjects, pharmacology for instance, it is not difficult to structure unambiguous MCQs, whereas in clinical anaesthesia where things are less clear cut and exceptions abound, the setting of questions is less easy. Take this into account, trust the examiner and do not look for ambiguities and difficulties that do not exist. Some candidates read the questions as if they are legal experts and quote obscure references to justify their answer. Forget it, take the questions at face value, do not look for difficulties that are not there.

QUESTION STRUCTURE

"The type of question used is the same throughout all parts of the FCAnaes examination and consists of a stem and five completions (branches), each of which in conjunction with the stem is either a true or a false statement. You may state for each response whether it is true or false."

Take care not to let your answer to one branch influence your answers to the other branches. Re-read the stem each time in conjunction with the individual branch as a complete statement. If this is not done it is easy to make errors, especially in situations where negatives are used in either the stem or branch, or worst of all if there are negatives in both.

MARKING

"Candidates receive +1 mark for each correctly answered response, −1 for each response incorrectly answered and 0 if no attempt is made to answer. A "don't know" box is included on the answer sheet." Therefore the maximum for each question if all 5 are right is +5, and if all incorrect the minimum is −5.

A raw score is then worked out from the total number of the correct true or false answers, less the total number of incorrect true or false answers, this raw score could be negative. The corrected percentage score on which most assessment is based, is the raw score multiplied by 100 and divided by the maximum possible score, which in this exam is 300. Deciding which candidates pass, can be done in terms of a specific pass mark or in terms of rank (their position in the group). It is debatable which is being used in this exam. The knowledge that the proportion of people passing changes little, suggests that rank is more important but if this were so then should the overall standard of candidates' performance improve, the exam effectively becomes harder. It is known that 'discriminator questions' are used, these are questions that have been set previously and the candidate's performance in these can be compared with their use on previous occasions. On the basis of this the pass mark for the whole exam can be adjusted to compensate for any variation in the overall ease or difficulty of the remaining questions. There are probably elements of both methods being used in deciding who passes and who fails.

PASS MARK
The MCQ paper acts as a screen, "candidates whose performance in the multiple choice question paper of the Part 1 examination is very poor will be debarred from the oral examination." Probably about 10–15% of candidates are excluded in this way. It would seem that the pass mark generally lies around 55% to 60% and making allowance for the fact that a variable proportion of one's answers will be wrong, it seems unlikely that a candidate will pass if less than 200 answers are filled in on the computer card. For those not excluded from the rest of the exam on their MCQ performance alone, there is always the opportunity of improving a marginal MCQ mark with a good performance in the rest of the examination.

GUESSING
Wild guesses should be randomly correct or incorrect and should lead to a score of zero, so guessing is unlikely to improve your score. There is however what can be called the informed guess or hunch, it is generally agreed that if you are only moderately sure of an answer it usually better to follow your hunch rather than to leave the question unanswered.

WORDING OF QUESTIONS
It cannot be said too often that it is vital to read each question carefully, re-reading the stem with each branch. The questions have been worded with considerable care and each word is there for a reason. There are however certain 'weasel words' that often cause problems and should be treated with care. 'Always' and 'never' can rarely be used in relation to questions related to clinical problems and therefore words such as 'commonly', 'rarely', 'may' and suchlike abound in MCQ papers. Try not to let yourself become obsessed by them. Trust those who set the paper and do not look for tricks. If a question seems ambiguous and you are genuinely confused by the wording, an examiner is usually present at the examination and you should ask for clarification.

Good false answers are particularly difficult to devise, often they are based on the opposite of the right answer, look carefully to be sure that prefixes such as hyper- and hypo- are really correct. The genuine red herring can be difficult to check as one often feels that if you read widely enough you will find a reference showing it to be correct, but at the level of the Part 1 FCAnaes if it is not in the standard textbooks the answer can be taken as wrong.

FILLING IN THE ANSWERS

"At each examination you receive a question book detailing the questions and a printed lector sheet on which you mark your answers. You are not allowed to retain the question book. You are advised, in the examination instructions, to enter your answers in the question book first and then to transpose them to the lector sheet." The so-called lector sheet or computer card should be marked exactly according to the instructions and with great care. They are marked by being passed through an automatic document reader and untidiness can lead to the machine misreading the answer.

PLAN OF CAMPAIGN

Although everyone will have their own way of organising their time during the paper, we give here a suggested 'plan of campaign'. Whether or not you choose to use it, we believe that it is a good idea to consider it carefully so that you have thought about your own approach before you enter the examination hall.

1. Fill in your name, number and other details that are required on the computer card.

2. Go through the paper steadily doing the following:

    a) mark on the question paper the answers to those questions of which you are sure of the answer, by putting for instance a T for true and F for false against each branch
    b) put a line through any question if you feel that you have no clue about the subject or the correct answers
    c) put a question mark by the stem of the remaining questions, these are those that you believe you could answer given time to think about them.

3. Check the time and work out how much is left leaving aside at least half an hour to fill up the computer card, then count up the number of questions you have put a question mark by and work out how much time you can therefore spend on each question.

4. Go through the paper again trying to work out the answers to the marked questions but not spending more than the calculated proportion of time on any one.

5. Check the time, there should still be plenty left. Mark up the computer card exactly as instructed, double checking to ensure that you are doing so correctly. Mistakes can be made by getting out of phase between the number of the question in the paper and on the computer card, it is therefore sensible to mark up say five questions at a time and then check them to ensure that both the marking up and their numbers are correct. It is vital that the marking up on to the computer card is done correctly.

6. Finally, go back to any question that you felt you might have puzzled out with more time, but resist the temptation to change the answers to other questions unless you are absolutely sure that the original answer was wrong. Mark these on the computer card as you go.

Check once more that your name and number are on the computer card before handing it in. With an MCQ exam, if you feel you have done all the questions you can, it is best to leave the examination hall.

DISTRIBUTION OF QUESTIONS
Although guidance is given on the overall syllabus, the balance of questions in different areas is not detailed. We would suggest that in the MCQ paper the distribution is probably about:

> 20 anaesthetics
> 12 pharmacology
> 4 physics and clinical measurement
> 2 anatomy
> 12 physiology
> 10 medicine and surgery

This has been used as the basis of the test MCQ papers in this book.

HOW TO USE THE MCQ PAPERS IN THIS BOOK

We suggest that you work through each of these sets of 60 multiple choice questions as if it were a real examination. To do this you should spend no more than 90 minutes on each, this will ensure that sufficient time is allowed in the real examination to fill in the answers on the computer cards. Try to reproduce examination conditions as closely as possible by being sure you will not be disturbed and resisting any temptation to obtain help from books.

As you work through each question be sure to mark your answer against the space by the A. . . B. . . C. . . D. . . E. . . at the bottom, using 'T' for True and 'F' for False. When you have completed the paper you can then mark it by using the answers at the back of the book. If you wish you can give yourself +1 for each correct answer and −1 for each incorrect answer and thus work out your raw score and corrected percentage score as previously described.

Rather than worrying too much about your score, the explanations should be used to identify and remedy any gaps in your knowledge.

MCQ : PRACTICE EXAM 1

60 Questions: Time allowed 2 hours
Indicate your answers by writing T for True and F for False
in the spaces provided.

1. **Features of an anaphylactic reaction to thiopentone include**

    A   periorbital oedema
    B   petechial rash
    C   marked hypotension
    D   bronchospasm
    E   a fall in the circulating levels of IgE

    Your answers: A.......B.......C.......D.......E.......

2. **Plasma protein solutions (PPF, HAS)**

    A   are stored at room temperature
    B   are prepared from pooled plasma and so may transmit hepatitis
        virus to the recipient
    C   contain not less than 4.3 g/dl of protein
    D   are used in the treatment of disseminated intravascular
        coagulation
    E   contain approximately 145 mmol/l of sodium

    Your answers: A.......B.......C.......D.......E.......

3. **The following anaesthetic induction agents commonly cause thrombosis on intravenous injection:**

    A   thiopentone
    B   etomidate
    C   methohexitone
    D   diazepam in propylene glycol
    E   propofol

    Your answers: A.......B.......C.......D.......E.......

4. **Recognised complications of supraclavicular brachial plexus block include**

    A   intravascular administration of local anaesthetic
    B   pneumothorax
    C   vagal block
    D   phrenic nerve block
    E   Horner's syndrome

    Your answers: A.......B.......C.......D.......E.......

11

5. **Gastric emptying is delayed by**

    A   trauma
    B   anxiety
    C   morphine
    D   metoclopramide
    E   ranitidine

    Your answers: A.......B.......C.......D.......E.......

6. **Soda lime**

    A   is mainly calcium carbonate
    B   can be used to scavenge nitrous oxide
    C   needs water to absorb carbon dioxide
    D   in a properly packed canister half the volume should be space
        between the granules
    E   gets hot in use

    Your answers: A.......B.......C.......D.......E.......

7. **An adult who does not breathe for 1 hour after 50 mg suxa-methonium**

    A   is likely to be a homozygote for an abnormal gene responsible
        for cholinesterase
    B   is likely to have malignant hyperthermia
    C   may be hypokalaemic
    D   should be given a blood transfusion to raise his cholinesterase
        level
    E   should be treated with intravenous neostigmine

    Your answers: A.......B.......C.......D.......E.......

8. **A patient 4 hours postoperatively shows the following: BP 170/100, pulse 100, warm periphery, arterial blood gases on air PCO_2 9.0 kPa, PO_2 9.0 kPa and bicarbonate 28 mmol/l, this may be due to**

    A   segmental pulmonary collapse
    B   septicaemia
    C   overtransfusion
    D   underventilation
    E   metabolic acidosis

    Your answers: A.......B.......C.......D.......E.......

9. **In lignocaine overdosage, the following may occur:**

    A unconsciousness
    B hypotension
    C involuntary movements
    D bronchospasm
    E hypothermia

    Your answers: A.......B.......C.......D.......E.......

10. **Warming blood to 37°C for massive blood transfusion**

    A reduces the incidence of infection
    B increases the CO_2 tension
    C reduces the O_2 tension
    D shifts the oxygen dissociation curve to the right
    E reduces the incidence of arrhythmias

    Your answers: A.......B.......C.......D.......E.......

11. **The following are useful in the treatment of bronchospasm occurring during general anaesthesia:**

    A aminophylline
    B propranolol
    C salbutamol
    D disodium cromoglycate
    E halothane

    Your answers: A.......B.......C.......D.......E.......

12. **Measures taken to minimise heat loss during surgery include**

    A operating theatre temperature of 20°C
    B use of space blankets
    C giving fluids into a central vein
    D humidifying inspired gases
    E small doses of phenothiazines

    Your answers: A.......B.......C.......D.......E.......

13. **Intubation of the right main bronchus with unchanged ventilation may in the first 5 minutes, lead to**

    A hypotension
    B hypercapnia
    C an increased requirement for an insoluble anaesthetic agent
    D collapse of the right upper lobe
    E hypoxaemia

Your answers: A.......B.......C.......D.......E......

14. **Depolarising block may be produced by**

    A suxamethonium
    B neostigmine
    C atracurium
    D vecuronium
    E edrophonium

Your answers: A.......B.......C.......D.......E......

15. **Severely obese patients may be**

    A hypoxaemic
    B difficult to intubate
    C unusually sensitive to non-depolarising muscle relaxants
    D unusually sensitive to thiopentone
    E hypercarbic

Your answers: A.......B.......C.......D.......E......

16. **When testing a modern anaesthetic machine, prior to use**

    A the pipelines should remain connected at all times
    B disconnection of nitrous oxide supply prevents the functioning of the oxygen failure alarm
    C all vaporisers should be turned on
    D occluding the anaesthetic gas outlet should lead to the pressure blow off valve opening
    E Bodock seals should be replaced each day

Your answers: A.......B.......C.......D.......E......

17. **Signs of the muscle relaxant wearing off during anaesthesia with IPPV include**

    A   a rise in pulse rate
    B   swallowing
    C   sweating
    D   hiccup
    E   an increase in inflation pressure on a volume cycled ventilator

    Your answers: A.......B.......C.......D.......E.......

18. **At equivalent MAC, comparing halothane with enflurane**

    A   enflurane causes more respiratory depression than halothane
    B   enflurane causes more cardiac arrhythmias than halothane
    C   enflurane causes a greater fall in cardiac output than halothane
    D   similar amounts of inorganic fluoride are produced in the metabolism of both agents
    E   enflurane has a higher boiling point than halothane

    Your answers: A.......B.......C.......D.......E.......

19. **The following are true of intravenous regional anaesthesia:**

    A   it was first described by Carl August Bier in 1908 using lignocaine
    B   in the arm a cannula for the injection of local anaesthetic may safely be placed in the antecubital fossa
    C   the tourniquet should be inflated to 30 mmHg above systolic pressure
    D   bupivacaine 0.125% is a suitable agent to use
    E   it should not be used in patients with sickle cell trait

    Your answers: A.......B.......C.......D.......E.......

20. **Following intravenous thiopentone, the following may occur:**

    A   severe hypotension
    B   respiratory depression
    C   liver toxicity
    D   increased intracranial pressure
    E   epileptic convulsions

    Your answers: A.......B.......C.......D.......E.......

21. **Dantrolene**

    A   stimulates respiration
    B   has skeletal muscle relaxant properties
    C   is a narcotic antagonist
    D   is useful prophylactically in the management of malignant hyperthermia
    E   can antagonise myoneural blockers

    Your answers: A.......B.......C.......D.......E.......

22. **Digoxin is indicated in**

    A   atrial flutter
    B   2:1 block
    C   ventricular tachycardia
    D   nodal tachycardia
    E   Stokes-Adams attacks

    Your answers: A.......B.......C.......D.......E.......

23. **Dopamine infused at a dosage of 10 μg/kg/minute would produce**

    A   increased urinary output
    B   increased sodium excretion
    C   increased cardiac output
    D   multiple ventricular extrasystoles
    E   an unchanged peripheral resistance

    Your answers: A.......B.......C.......D.......E.......

24. **The blood glucose may be lowered by**

    A   isoprenaline
    B   growth hormone
    C   metformin
    D   glucagon
    E   glibenclamide

    Your answers: A.......B.......C.......D.......E.......

25. Atracurium

   A may release histamine
   B is metabolised to laudanosine
   C is contraindicated in anephric patients
   D is an ester
   E is miscible with thiopentone

Your answers: A.......B.......C.......D.......E.......

26. Alfentanil

   A decreases sensitivity of the respiratory centre to carbon dioxide
   B has a shorter half-life than fentanyl
   C relaxes uterine muscle
   D causes severe myocardial depression
   E is twice as potent as fentanyl

Your answers: A.......B.......C.......D.......E.......

27. The following are true of thiopentone:

   A the pH of a 2.5% solution is 6.8
   B less than 15% of an administered dose is metabolised each hour
   C it is the sulphur analogue of pentobarbitone
   D it is more than 50% protein bound
   E it exists in the plasma in both ionised and non-ionised forms

Your answers: A.......B.......C.......D.......E.......

28. In comparison with atropine, hyoscine

   A is more anti-emetic
   B induces more tachycardia
   C is more sedative
   D is a more effective anti-sialogogue
   E has a greater anti-Parkinsonian action

Your answers: A.......B.......C.......D.......E.......

29. **Depolarising muscle blockade with suxamethonium is characterised by**

A   potentiation by neostigmine
B   antagonism with d-tubocurarine
C   fade
D   post-tetanic facilitation
E   antagonism by lowering body temperature

Your answers: A.......B.......C.......D.......E.......

30. **Bupivacaine**

A   produces depolarisation in the neural membrane of peripheral nerves
B   is detoxified in the liver
C   is an ester
D   can cause methaemoglobinaemia
E   30 ml of 0.5% solution is the recommended maximum dose in a fit 75 kg man

Your answers: A.......B.......C.......D.......E.......

31. **Doxapram**

A   stimulates respiration by an effect on central chemoreceptors
B   increases whole body oxygen consumption
C   reverses both the respiratory and analgesic effects of narcotics
D   may cause convulsions
E   is metabolised by cholinesterase

Your answers: A.......B.......C.......D.......E.......

32. **Ketamine is contraindicated**

A   as an induction agent in the asthmatic patient
B   as an induction agent in emergency anaesthesia of the shocked patient
C   for anaesthesia in the patient with facial burns
D   in hypertensive patients
E   as an induction agent for caesarean section

Your answers: A.......B.......C.......D.......E.......

33. The accuracy of a rotameter may be affected by

A dirt on the bobbin
B static electricity
C passing the wrong gas through it
D back pressure from a Manley ventilator
E using it at high altitude

Your answers: A.......B.......C.......D.......E.......

34. Concerning fires and explosions in theatre

A the relative humidity in theatre should be about 66%
B air is safer than oxygen
C switches in the 'zone of risk' should be spark-proof
D the floor should be terrazzo on a well conducting screed
E cotton fabrics are better than wool

Your answers: A.......B.......C.......D.......E.......

35. Critical temperature

A of nitrous oxide is 36.5°C
B is the temperature below which a gas cannot be liquefied by pressure
C separates gases from vapours
D of oxygen is −182.5°C
E is always lower than the boiling point of the same gas

Your answers: A.......B.......C.......D.......E.......

36. The following are true for gases in cylinders:

A nitrous oxide and entonox are filled to the same pressure
B a full oxygen cylinder is at a pressure of 1950 kPa
C nitrous oxide should contain 1% water vapour
D nitrous oxide should not be stored below −8°C
E size E cylinders of oxygen and nitrous oxide are generally used on a Boyles machine

Your answers: A.......B.......C.......D.......E.......

37. **The epidural space is bounded by the**

    A sacrococcygeal membrane
    B anterior longitudinal ligament
    C posterior surface of the lamina
    D interspinous ligament
    E intervertebral foramen

    Your answers: A.......B.......C.......D.......E.......

38. **Block of the cervical sympathetic ganglia produces**

    A dilatation of the conjunctival vessels
    B anhydrosis of the ipsilateral face
    C miosis
    D nasal congestion
    E exophthalmos

    Your answers: A.......B.......C.......D.......E.......

39. **Carbon monoxide**

    A has 150 times greater affinity for haemoglobin than oxygen
    B stimulates the chemoreceptors
    C in smokers can combine with up to 15% of the haemoglobin
    D is rapidly eliminated by breathing high oxygen concentrations
    E shifts the oxygen dissociation curve to the left

    Your answers: A.......B.......C.......D.......E.......

40. **The calibre of the bronchi increases**

    A in response to stimulation of their parasympathetic nerve
       supply
    B during inspiration
    C in response to β-receptor stimulation of their smooth
       muscle
    D during coughing
    E in response to histamine

    Your answers: A.......B.......C.......D.......E.......

41. **The following statements concerning oxygenation are correct:**

A the PO_2 of air in the trachea is less than that in room air because it contains saturated water vapour
B alveolar PO_2 is the same as PO_2 of air in the trachea
C mixed venous PO_2 is normally 5.3 kPa (40 mmHg)
D hypercarbia may cause cyanosis
E one of the causes of A-a PO_2 gradient in normal people is anatomical shunt

Your answers: A.......B.......C.......D.......E.......

42. **Arterial carbon dioxide tension**

A is normally 0.8 kPa (6 mmHg) lower than mixed venous CO_2 tension
B does not affect plasma bicarbonate concentration
C rises when living at an altitude of 5000 metres
D rises during sleep
E falls to half its original value if alveolar ventilation is doubled and CO_2 production remains constant

Your answers: A.......B.......C.......D.......E.......

43. **Respiratory changes during pregnancy include**

A decrease in functional residual capacity
B increase in airways resistance
C decreased arterial PCO_2
D increased tidal volume
E increased minute volume

Your answers: A.......B.......C.......D.......E.......

44. **The total peripheral resistance of the systemic circulation**

A is higher than that of the pulmonary circulation
B rises during pregnancy
C is higher during exercise than at rest
D is lower than normal during vasovagal syncope
E falls with isoflurane at 1 MAC

Your answers: A.......B.......C.......D.......E.......

45. **In a normal heart, cardiac output**

    A   varies with oxygen consumption
    B   rises when the end diastolic volume increases
    C   rises with increased afterload
    D   rises with increased myocardial contractility
    E   can be measured by echocardiography

    Your answers: A.......B........C.......D.......E.......

46. **An increase in vagal activity results in the following changes in the heart:**

    A   a decrease in rate
    B   an increase in contractility
    C   a decrease in the rate of repolarisation of the pacemaker cells
    D   a prolongation of conduction at the AV node
    E   an increased cardiac output

    Your answers: A.......B.......C.......D.......E.......

47. **The cerebrospinal fluid**

    A   has a higher glucose content than plasma
    B   has a higher pH than plasma
    C   has a higher protein content than plasma
    D   has a total volume of approximately 250 ml
    E   is secreted from the arachnoid villi

    Your answers: A.......B.......C.......D.......E.......

48. **The acute loss of more than 500 ml of blood in the adult results in the following effects:**

    A   severe vasoconstriction in the cerebral circulation
    B   a reduction of the glomerular filtration rate
    C   increased aldosterone secretion
    D   increased rate of discharge from the arterial baroreceptors
    E   reduced ADH production

    Your answers: A.......B.......C.......D.......E.......

49. Cerebral blood flow will be increased by

A   a rise in arterial PCO_2 to 8 kPa (60 mmHg)
B   a head down posture
C   an increase in systemic BP from 110 to 130 mmHg
D   hyperventilation
E   a rise in arterial PO_2

Your answers: A.......B.......C......D.......E.......

50. In the normal heart

A   blood in the left atrium contains less oxygen than blood in the pulmonary artery
B   right ventricular pressure might be 25/10 mmHg
C   pulmonary artery systolic pressure is usually about 10 mmHg less than right ventricular systolic pressure
D   left ventricular pressure might be 125/3 mmHg
E   blood in the pulmonary artery has an oxygen saturation of 75%

Your answers: A.......B.......C......D.......E.......

51. Down's Syndrome is associated with

A   atrial septal defects
B   trisomy of chromosome 21
C   leukaemia
D   webbing of the neck
E   constriction of the nasal passages

Your answers: A.......B.......C......D.......E.......

52. In gastro-intestinal obstruction

A   the fluid deficit may exceed 10% of the body weight
B   metabolic acidosis may develop due to prolonged vomiting
C   epidural anaesthesia may increase the risk of bowel rupture
D   electrolyte disturbances may predispose to cardiac irregularity
E   abdominal distension may embarrass respiration

Your answers: A.......B.......C......D.......E.......

53. **Angina pectoris is a recognised feature of**

   A   aortic stenosis
   B   anaemia
   C   polyarteritis
   D   myxoedema
   E   paroxysmal ventricular tachycardia

Your answers: A.......B.......C.......D.......E.......

54. **Glycine 1.5% used for irrigation during trans-urethral prostatectomy (TURP) can cause**

   A   hyponatraemia
   B   hypercalcaemia
   C   haemolysis
   D   hyperkalaemia
   E   haemodilution

Your answers: A.......B.......C.......D.......E.......

55. **A prolonged prothrombin time is found in**

   A   haemolytic jaundice
   B   liver failure
   C   adrenal failure
   D   factor VII deficiency
   E   malabsorption with steatorrhoea

Your answers: A.......B.......C.......D.......E.......

56. **Chronic deficiency of hormones of the adrenal cortex is associated with**

   A   low serum sodium
   B   the appearance of striae on the abdomen
   C   low blood pressure
   D   loss of pigmentation
   E   low serum potassium

Your answers: A.......B.......C.......D.......E.......

57. **Chronic bronchitis is characterised by**

   A   air trapping in the alveolae
   B   increased mucus secretion
   C   a reduced residual volume
   D   a normal ratio between forced expiratory volume (FEV_1) and forced vital capacity (FVC)
   E   maximum life expectancy of 10 years

   Your answers: A.......B.......C.......D.......E.......

58. **The incidence of deep venous thrombosis is increased by**

   A   bed rest
   B   anaemia
   C   neoplastic disease
   D   obesity
   E   epidural anaesthesia

   Your answers: A.......B.......C.......D.......E.......

59. **In chronic iron deficiency anaemia**

   A   the PO_2 of arterial blood is lower than normal
   B   mean corpuscular volume is normal
   C   blood transfusion produces immediate improvement in tissue oxygenation
   D   target cells are present
   E   alkalosis is hazardous because it shifts the O_2 dissociation curve to the left

   Your answers: A.......B.......C.......D.......E.......

60. **In comparison with patients suffering mainly from emphysema (pink puffers), those whose disease is primarily due to chronic bronchitis (blue bloaters) have a**

   A   lower arterial PCO_2
   B   higher standard bicarbonate
   C   lower haematocrit
   D   lower arterial PO_2
   E   lower diffusing capacity for carbon monoxide (transfer factor)

   Your answers: A.......B.......C.......D.......E.......

END OF PRACTICE EXAM 1

Go over your answers until your time is up.
Answers and explanations are on page 89.

60 Questions: Time allowed 2 hours
Indicate your answers by writing T for True and F for False
in the spaces provided.

1. **Side-effects of epidural morphine include**

    A   retention of urine
    B   respiratory depression
    C   muscle weakness
    D   itching
    E   nausea and vomiting

    Your answers: A.......B.......C.......D.......E.......

2. **Convulsions occurring intraoperatively or in the early postoperative period may be due to**

    A   ether
    B   suxamethonium
    C   halothane
    D   bupivacaine
    E   hypoxia

    Your answers: A.......B.......C.......D.......E.......

3. **The Magill circuit**

    A   is an example of a Mapleson A circuit
    B   is functionally similar to the Lack circuit
    C   is suitable for children over 25 kg
    D   is suitable for IPPV
    E   rebreathing and hypercarbia will occur if the fresh gas flow is
        less than the minute volume

    Your answers: A.......B.......C.......D.......E.......

4. **Following intra-arterial thiopentone**

    A   permanent damage does not occur with a 2.5% solution
    B   pain is due to release of histamine from the vessel wall
    C   stellate ganglion block is part of the management
    D   damage only follows injection into the brachial artery
    E   onset of unconsciousness is delayed

    Your answers: A.......B.......C.......D.......E.......

5. **Useful tests of clinically adequate return of muscle power after neuromuscular block include**

   A   head lift sustained for 5 seconds
   B   measurement of tidal volume
   C   measurement of minute volume
   D   measurement of end tidal CO_2
   E   assessing the response to airway obstruction

   Your answers: A.......B.......C.......D.......E.......

6. **The following are true in relation to caudal block:**

   A   it is an extradural injection through the sacrococcygeal membrane
   B   the dura extends down to the lower border of L5
   C   it causes some parasympathetic blockade
   D   bupivacaine 0.25%, 0.5 ml/kg is a suitable dose for children having circumcision under general anaesthesia
   E   the average capacity of the sacral canal is 24 ml in adult males

   Your answers: A.......B.......C.......D.......E.......

7. **In Guedel's classification of the depth of anaesthesia**

   A   there are four stages
   B   there are 4 planes in stage 3
   C   the classification was based on open ether and spontaneous respiration
   D   in stage 2 respiration is regular
   E   the pupils are small in stage 2

   Your answers: A.......B.......C.......D.......E.......

8. **In nitrous oxide cylinders for medical use**

   A   the cylinder is initially full of liquid
   B   nitrous oxide is produced by heating ammonium nitrate
   C   contaminants may be tested for with moistened starch-iodide paper
   D   in continuous use the gauge pressure will only fall when the cylinder is nearly empty
   E   contamination with nitric oxide may occur

   Your answers: A.......B.......C.......D.......E.......

9. **A patient with rheumatoid arthritis who is scheduled for hip surgery is likely to be**

A   in cardiac failure
B   anaemic
C   difficult to intubate
D   difficult to venepuncture
E   hypotensive

Your answers: A.......B.......C.......D.......E.......

10. **Which of the following pathology results should lead to postponement of a routine operation and further investigation:**

A   haemoglobin 10.8 g/dl
B   glycosuria
C   serum potassium 5.0 mmol/l
D   porphyrinuria
E   bilirubin 15 μmol/l

Your answers: A.......B.......C.......D.......E.......

11. **A tourniquet to achieve a bloodless field for surgery of the lower limb**

A   should not be inflated for more than one hour
B   should be inflated to 50 mmHg above the systolic blood pressure
C   is associated with an increased risk of postoperative deep vein thrombosis
D   should not be used under spinal anaesthesia
E   is contraindicated in the presence of HbS

Your answers: A.......B.......C.......D.......E.......

12. **In an elderly patient with a fractured hip who is in poor health**

A   it is reasonable to delay the operation for 7–10 days
B   the most common cause of death is pulmonary embolism
C   the choice of anaesthetic technique has no bearing on post-operative mortality in the first two weeks
D   clinically significant arterial hypoxaemia follows any anaesthetic technique
E   spinal block to T10 is adequate

Your answers: A.......B.......C.......D.......E.......

13. **Factors predisposing to passive regurgitation of gastric contents include**

    A   a nasogastric tube
    B   hiatus hernia
    C   metoclopramide
    D   non-depolarising relaxants
    E   neostigmine

    Your answers: A.......B.......C.......D.......E.......

14. **Non-depolarising muscle relaxants**

    A   produce post-tetanic facilitation
    B   all have their action prolonged by alkalosis
    C   produce fasciculation
    D   can exhibit dual block
    E   have a prolonged action in severe hypothermia

    Your answers: A.......B.......C.......D.......E.......

15. **The level of serum potassium may be**

    A   increased by suxamethonium
    B   increased by thiopentone
    C   increased in metabolic alkalosis
    D   affected by extensive burns
    E   reduced by d-tubocurarine

    Your answers: A.......B.......C.......D.......E.......

16. **Fat embolism may produce**

    A   fat in the sputum
    B   fat in the urine
    C   petechial haemorrhages
    D   pyrexia
    E   respiratory distress

    Your answers: A.......B.......C.......D.......E.......

17. **The following may be useful in the management of malignant hyperpyrexia:**

    A   mannitol
    B   sodium EDTA
    C   sodium bicarbonate
    D   magnesium sulphate
    E   glucose and insulin

    Your answers: A.......B.......C.......D.......E.......

18. **A fit 50 year old man develops a slow nodal rhythm during halothane anaesthesia**

    A   this is dangerous and requires treatment
    B   this is often induced by a fall in blood pressure
    C   it may be due to hypoxia
    D   it is often associated with light anaesthesia
    E   this usually responds to intravenous atropine

    Your answers: A.......B.......C.......D.......E.......

19. **At concentrations normally used for clinical anaesthesia, halothane**

    A   is inflammable
    B   raises the intracranial pressure
    C   cannot be used in a closed circuit with soda lime
    D   sensitizes the heart to the effect of catecholamines
    E   relaxes the uterus

    Your answers: A.......B.......C.......D.......E.......

20. **Immediately following a large air embolus**

    A   end tidal CO_2 will fall
    B   a loud precordial murmur will be heard
    C   the blood pressure increases
    D   central venous pressure falls
    E   nitrous oxide should be discontinued

    Your answers: A.......B.......C.......D.......E.......

21. Atropine

A blocks the muscarinic effects of acetylcholine
B given as premedication is contraindicated in glaucoma
C crosses the blood brain barrier
D inhibits acetylcholine release
E can cause convulsions

Your answers: A.......B.......C.......D.......E.......

22. Isoflurane

A produces more myocardial depression than halothane
B undergoes 2% metabolism in the liver
C may produce seizures in epileptic patients
D is more potent than halothane
E has a MAC of 1.2% in oxygen

Your answers: A.......B.......C.......D.......E.......

23. The following occur in raw opium:

A heroin
B methadone
C papaverine
D thebaine
E codeine

Your answers: A.......B.......C.......D.......E.......

24. Chlorpromazine

A is a weak antihistamine
B is an α-blocker
C can cause Parkinsonism
D is an anti-emetic
E has an atropine-like action

Your answers: A.......B.......C.......D.......E.......

25. **The MAC value of an inhalational anaesthetic agent will be influenced by**

   A the age of the patient
   B the administration of morphine with it
   C a change in the arterial PCO_2 from 3.5 to 6.5 kPa (26 to 49 mmHg)
   D its blood/gas partition coefficient
   E the use of nitrous oxide with it

   Your answers: A.......B.......C.......D.......E.......

26. **Halothane decreases the blood pressure as a result of**

   A direct myocardial depression
   B a fall in total peripheral resistance
   C a central action on the vasomotor centre
   D ganglion blockade
   E increased aldosterone secretion

   Your answers: A.......B.......C.......D.......E.......

27. **The following are anticonvulsant:**

   A diazepam
   B chlormethiazole
   C oxazepam
   D chlorpropamide
   E thiopentone

   Your answers: A.......B.......C.......D.......E.......

28. **The following are examples of pharmacological calcium antagonists:**

   A verapamil
   B captopril
   C propranolol
   D nifedipine
   E hydralazine

   Your answers: A.......B.......C.......D.......E.......

29. **Recognised contraindications to thiopentone include**

    A constrictive pericarditis
    B sickle cell anaemia
    C porphyria
    D malignant hyperthermia
    E monoamine oxidase inhibitor drug therapy

Your answers: A.......B.......C.......D.......E.......

30. **Morphine**

    A may cause histamine release
    B decreases catecholamine levels
    C causes miosis
    D causes vomiting by direct stimulation of the vomiting centre
    E arterial PCO_2 is markedly raised with normal therapeutic dosage

Your answers: A.......B.......C.......D.......E.......

31. **Propranolol is contraindicated in**

    A bronchial asthma
    B the presence of a low serum potassium
    C paroxysmal nocturnal dyspnoea
    D patients already on digoxin
    E atrial fibrillation

Your answers: A.......B.......C.......D.......E.......

32. **Significant vasoconstriction occurs with**

    A cocaine
    B amethocaine
    C prilocaine
    D lignocaine
    E bupivacaine

Your answers: A.......B.......C.......D.......E.......

33. **The following may lead to over estimation of the blood pressure:**

    A   too wide a cuff
    B   too fat an arm and a standard cuff
    C   letting the cuff down too slowly
    D   having the syphgmomanometer above the patient
    E   severe atherosclerosis

    Your answers: A.......B.......C......D.......E.......

34. **The saturated vapour pressure of a liquid**

    A   is linearly related to temperature
    B   can exceed the normal atmospheric pressure
    C   is a function of barometric pressure
    D   maintains a constant percentage of the vapour in the gas phase
        in a closed space above the liquid irrespective of the total
        pressure
    E   is 7.6 kPa (57 mmHg) for water at 37°C

    Your answers: A.......B.......C.......D.......E.......

35. **For laminar flow in a tube, the flow rate is directly proportional to**

    A   its length
    B   the fourth power of its radius
    C   the density of the gas or liquid flowing through it
    D   the pressure drop across it
    E   the viscosity of the gas or liquid flowing through it

    Your answers: A.......B.......C......D.......E.......

36. **Helium has the following advantages over nitrogen for divers at
    depth:**

    A   it diffuses more rapidly into the body tissues
    B   it is denser
    C   it has a lower viscosity
    D   it has less narcotic effect
    E   it is a good insulator

    Your answers: A.......B.......C......D.......E.......

37. **The oesophagus**

    A lies within the anterior mediastinum
    B is lined by columnar epithelium
    C starts at the level of the sixth cervical vertebra
    D receives its motor nerve supply from the vagus
    E terminates about 20 cm from the teeth

    Your answers: A.......B.......C.......D.......E.......

38. **In relation to the first rib**

    A scalenus medius inserts into the scalene tubercle
    B the lower trunk of the brachial plexus lies on the upper surface
    C the subclavian artery lies in front of the scalene tubercle
    D the stellate ganglion lies anterior to its head
    E the subclavian vein lies behind the scalene tubercle

    Your answers: A.......B.......C.......D.......E.......

39. **A Valsalva manoeuvre**

    A is a forced expiration against a closed glottis or other airway
       obstruction
    B is initially associated with increased systolic arterial pressure
    C is associated with a decreased total peripheral resistance
    D is normally associated with a tachycardia
    E is normally followed by a bradycardia

    Your answers: A.......B.......C.......D.......E.......

40. **The sympathetic nervous system**

    A has no cholinergic postganglionic fibres
    B is inhibitory to the smooth muscle of the ileum
    C fibres may be blocked by guanethidine
    D has fibres in the vagus nerve
    E when stimulated causes miosis

    Your answers: A.......B.......C.......D.......E.......

41. **Erythropoietin**

   A   is formed in response to a high carbon dioxide tension
   B   is formed in response to hypoxia
   C   formation occurs in the kidney
   D   is a polysaccharide
   E   promotes the conversion of stem cells to haemocytoblasts

   Your answers: A.......B........C.......D.......E.......

42. **Carbon dioxide is transported in the blood**

   A   in the red cells
   B   as phosphate esters
   C   in simple solution
   D   combined with plasma protein
   E   as carbamino compound with haemoglobin

   Your answers: A.......B........C.......D.......E.......

43. **Acclimatisation to the hypoxia of high altitude results in**

   A   a decreased affinity of haemoglobin for oxygen
   B   a reduced arterial CO_2 level
   C   an increase in oxygen carrying capacity
   D   an increase in respiratory minute volume
   E   an increase in cardiac output

   Your answers: A.......B........C.......D.......E.......

44. **The following hormones are secreted by the anterior pituitary:**

   A   somatostatin
   B   oxytocin
   C   prolactin
   D   aldosterone
   E   thyrotropin

   Your answers: A.......B........C.......D.......E.......

45. **The haemoglobin oxygen dissociation curve is moved to the right by**

A   acidosis
B   raised body temperature
C   passage through the pulmonary capillaries
D   ageing
E   anaemia

Your answers: A.......B.......C.......D.......E.......

46. **In a recording of the central venous pressure**

A   the 'a' wave is caused by atrial systole
B   the 'c' wave is caused by bulging of the tricuspid valve during isometric ventricular contraction
C   the 'v' wave is due to atrial filling with the tricuspid valve closed
D   the pressure is increased during inspiration
E   the pressure is always raised if left atrial pressure is increased

Your answers: A.......B.......C.......D.......E.......

47. **The functional residual capacity (FRC)**

A   falls with age
B   falls under anaesthesia with spontaneous respiration
C   rises under anaesthesia with IPPV
D   when it is reduced, the difference between the alveolar and arterial oxygen tension is reduced
E   if it falls below closing volume, atelectasis will ensue

Your answers: A.......B.......C.......D.......E.......

48. **Concerning normal kidney function**

A   sodium is mainly reabsorbed from the proximal tubule
B   glucose is completely reabsorbed providing the plasma concentration is normal
C   the urinary content of potassium is controlled by the secretory activity of the distal convoluted tubular cells
D   metabolic acidosis provokes increased ammonium excretion
E   ADH secretion only occurs in states of dehydration

Your answers: A.......B.......C.......D.......E.......

49. **The respiratory centre**

   A   is situated in the medulla oblongata
   B   is inhibited during vomiting
   C   causes regular rhythmic contraction of the expiratory muscles
        during quiet breathing
   D   is directly stimulated by hypoxia
   E   is sensitive to alterations in blood pH

   Your answers: A.......B.......C.......D.......E.......

50. **The following are true in regard to arterial blood gases:**

   A   the normal hydrogen ion concentration is 100 nmol/l
   B   the normal standard bicarbonate is 32 mmol/l
   C   a PaO_2 of 10 kPa (75 mmHg) is normal for an 80 year old man
   D   the $PaCO_2$ is raised in hypothermia
   E   the base deficit is the number of mmol of bicarbonate per litre
        of blood, required to correct the pH to 7.4 at a PCO_2 of 5.3
        kPa (40 mmHg) and 37°C

   Your answers: A.......B.......C.......D.......E.......

51. **Coma in a diabetic patient is more likely to be hypoglycaemic than
    ketotic if there is**

   A   dryness of the skin and tongue
   B   a history of abdominal pain
   C   a bilateral extensor plantar response
   D   hypotension
   E   Cushing's syndrome

   Your answers: A.......B.......C.......D.......E.......

52. **Increased skin pigmentation may be found in**

   A   myxoedema
   B   Addison's disease
   C   vitiligo
   D   pregnancy
   E   Cushing's syndrome

   Your answers: A.......B.......C.......D.......E.......

53. **A chronic bronchitic who normally has an arterial PCO_2 of 8.0 kPa (60 mmHg) and an arterial PO_2 of 8.0 kPa is found to have the following arterial blood gases: pH 7.29, PCO_2 8.26 kPa (62 mmHg), PO_2 8.13 kPa (61 mmHg), HCO_3 29.6 mmol/l, BE +0.5, SBC 24.5 mmol/l**

   A   he has an acidosis due to recent worsening of his bronchitis (acute on chronic)
   B   he has developed metabolic acidosis
   C   he could not have a metabolic acidosis with a BE of +0.5
   D   these are normal blood gases for him
   E   he has metabolic and respiratory alkalosis

   Your answers: A.......B.......C.......D.......E.......

54. **A long-standing, uncomplicated transection of the spinal cord at the level of C5 results in**

   A   flaccid paralysis of the legs
   B   loss of a shivering reflex
   C   loss of a micturition reflex
   D   hyperkalaemia with suxamethonium administration
   E   absence of sweat gland activity below the level of the lesion

   Your answers: A.......B.......C.......D.......E.......

55. **The following are features of Fallot's Tetralogy:**

   A   squatting
   B   syncopal attacks
   C   systolic bruit due to ventricular septal defect
   D   pulmonary oligaemia
   E   cyanosis aggravated by exertion

   Your answers: A.......B.......C.......D.......E.......

56. **A 60 year old man requires laparotomy for a perforated peptic ulcer. Recognised features include**

   A   an increased risk of inhalation of gastric contents
   B   metabolic acidosis
   C   hypercapnia
   D   increased bleeding due to thrombocytopenia
   E   raised serum amylase

   Your answers: A.......B.......C.......D.......E.......

57. In patients with sickle cell trait (heterozygotes)

A a Sickledex test will allow differentiation from homozygotes
B moderate anaemia is usually present
C episodic haematuria may be seen
D splenomegaly is a characteristic finding
E exchange transfusion may be necessary for major thoracic surgery

Your answers: A.......B.......C.......D.......E.......

58. In digoxin toxicity

A the ECG characteristically shows widespread RST segment depression
B intravenous calcium gluconate may temporarily reverse the toxic effects on the myocardium
C phenytoin may be helpful in the treatment of supraventricular dysrhythmias
D corticosteroids may restore normal conduction if heart block is present
E the plasma digoxin level is a reliable guide to severity

Your answers: A.......B.......C.......D.......E.......

59. Blood for transfusion is tested for

A syphilis
B brucellosis
C HIV antibody
D hepatitis A
E malaria

Your answers: A.......B.......C.......D.......E.......

60. ECG changes in hyperkalaemia include

A prominent P waves
B prominent T waves
C prominent U waves
D increased QRS duration
E a shortened PR interval

Your answers: A.......B.......C.......D.......E.......

END OF PRACTICE EXAM 2

**Go over your answers until your time is up.
Answers and explanations are on page 104.**

THE WRITTEN PAPER

The Guide states
"Unlike the MCQ, the written answer papers are designed not only to test accurate recall of the facts but also to give an indication of your ability to select the most relevant pieces of information, to assign relative importance to each and to assemble them logically. Tabulated telegraphic answers in which the correct information is randomly located within material of doubtful relevance are not necessarily, therefore, of a pass standard."

DISTRIBUTION OF QUESTIONS
The balance of questions that can be expected is

1. Anatomy – often includes a local anaesthetic block
2. Medicine or surgery
3. Therapeutics – usually pharmacology of anaesthetic drugs
4. 'Physics' – anaesthetic apparatus and monitoring
5. Physiology
6. Anaesthetic clinical practice
7. Anaesthetic clinical practice

Short note questions with three separate parts have been included.

DOING THE PAPER
The general advice for written papers is straightforward. Read the questions carefully a number of times. Underline the keywords. Start listing the topics you intend to include in your answer. Begin writing with a question you feel confident about to get in the correct frame of mind. Do not spend more than the right proportion of time on any one question. Keep asking yourself 'Am I answering the question?'. In an anaesthetic exam always consider if the question could include local as well as general anaesthesia? Keep adding to your list of topics for the questions you are less sure about, often things will come to mind as you are answering other questions. Read through your answers.

This is a 'Written Answer Paper' rather than an 'Essay Paper' and although this gives latitude for the use of headings and note form answers, you should still ensure that what you commit to paper is well laid out and has a logical sequence when read. "Discuss" should contain discussion and comparison. "Anaesthetic management" means everything an anaesthetist would be expected to do in relation to a case from the ward onwards. "Operative management" means the anaesthetist's management in the operating theatre from induction onwards. Diagrams can be used but be sure they are well drawn and labelled. Lists are best used only if time is desperately short. Selective underlining can be helpful but should not be over done. Keep sentences short and not more than two or three points in each paragraph.

"With the use of the close-marking system, failure to attempt the required number of questions will result in failure to pass the examination." The Guide thus makes it clear that it is essential to do all seven questions and a uniform standard of answers is required – one bad answer is almost certain to wreck the candidates chances however good the other questions may be. 20–25 minutes is the maximum time that should be allowed for writing on any one question if sufficient time is to be allowed for planning answers and reading through at the end.

"Written answers are also a test of your ability to communicate clearly and unambiguously and thus legibility and a reasonable command of the English language are of relevance." Bad spelling always irritates the examiner and poor writing wastes his time which is worse. It is usually better to write less and make sure that it is easy to read. If the writing is illegible the paper is sent to other examiners, if they too cannot read it the candidate fails.

Three Written Papers are set out in this section. It is suggested that you should do the Written Papers in as close to examination conditions as possible. Outline answers are provided later in the book to help to ensure that your factual content is complete but you are advised to show your answers to more senior colleagues to gain their opinion, particularly with regard to your layout and style.

WRITTEN PAPER 1

Time allowed 3 hours.

Candidates MUST answer ALL questions and are advised that the omission of any question is likely to result in failure to pass the paper.

1. Describe the anatomical structures encountered in the passage of a needle for spinal anaesthesia.

2. Describe the physiological effects of passive hyperventilation.

3. A patient with chronic bronchitis is to have a general anaesthetic, what tests of respiratory function would be of value and what would be the significance of the results obtained?

4. What are the actions of intravenous barbiturates on the cardio-vascular system? Discuss briefly their clinical significance.

5. What are the indications for awake intubation in the adult? Describe the local anaesthetic technique that you would use for this procedure.

6. Describe your anaesthetic management of a 25 year old woman, who is 35 weeks pregnant and has developed appendicitis.

7. Discuss the causes and treatment of a sudden rise in blood pressure during general anaesthesia for a laparotomy.

WRITTEN PAPER 2

Time allowed 3 hours.

Candidates MUST answer ALL questions and are advised that the omission of any question is likely to result in failure to pass the paper.

1. Describe the anatomical structures below the epiglottis seen during bronchoscopy.

2. Describe the physiological mechanisms by which arterial hypoxaemia may occur.

3. Describe briefly the physical principles involved in the functioning of calibrated anaesthetic vaporisers.

4. Compare and contrast the pharmacological effects of vecuronium and d-tubocurarine.

5. Describe in detail the management of intravenous regional anaesthesia (Bier's block) in the upper limb.

6. A woman in shock is thought to have an ectopic pregnancy, describe briefly your anaesthetic management.

7. How may hypercarbia develop during anaesthesia, what clinical changes may result?

WRITTEN PAPER 3

Time allowed 3 hours.

Candidates MUST answer ALL questions and are advised that the omission of any question is likely to result in failure to pass the paper.

1. Describe the relations of the internal jugular vein, what are the common complications of internal jugular cannulation.

2. Compare the physiological response to the infusion of 1 litre of normal saline with that resulting from the infusion of 1 litre of plasma.

3. Describe the Mapleson classification for anaesthetic circuits indicating to which group the circuits in common use belong.

4. What is the safe maximum dose of the commonly used local anaesthetic drugs? What may occur clinically with overdosage?

5. Discuss the advantages and disadvantages of spinal and general anaesthesia for a patient requiring surgery for a fractured neck of femur.

6. Discuss the problems posed for the anaesthetist by patients with narcotic addiction.

7. What action would you take when you find yourself unexpectedly unable to intubate a patient at emergency Caesarean section.

THE ORALS

Vivas probably engender more nervousness amongst candidates than any other part of the examination. While it is almost impossible to pass a viva with no knowledge, it is quite easy to fail one, despite reasonable knowledge, by poor technique. There are two vivas in this exam: a traditional oral and a clinical oral.

The Oral
Half an hour with two examiners. There is no doubt that the best antidote to nervousness is a broad base of knowledge: the feeling that whatever you are asked you would at least know something about the subject. Vivas are like climbing a tree. The first question is usually straight forward: the main trunk. One then explores main branches and then small branches, finally (provided you have answered correctly) on to small twigs at which point you fall off. The only thing candidates remember is the obscure twig they fell off. They do not remember that in getting there they answered many more important things correctly.

The examiner is trying to get an idea of the breadth of your knowledge and once he sees that you know about a topic will switch, often abruptly, to another. Candidates often comment afterwards on the amount of ground covered. It is tempting to try and spin out one topic if you know about it for fear of being asked something you do not know. This is usually a mistake. The more knowledge you can display on different topics the better.

We have not attempted to give practice vivas in this book, but here are a few hints on preparing yourself.

Practice
Get your consultant to give you a few practice vivas, so that you can improve your technique and build up confidence. Many candidates fail to do themselves justice through nervousness and unfamiliarity. Try to relax and speak audibly. Think before blurting out the first thing that comes into your head. Always start with common things. Remember that any anaesthetic starts with a preoperative visit. If asked how to manage an asthmatic for a vaginal hysterectomy, do not leap in with an epidural before assessing the patient.

Listen to the question
It is very irritating for examiners if you answer a question you were not asked. If asked "How would you anaesthetise a fit young man for a hernia", say what you usually do. If on the other hand the question is "What are the possible techniques of anaesthesia for herniorrhaphy" list the different techniques, do not say "My consultant always paralyses and ventilates them".

Leading the examiner or digging a pit

Most of the time the examiner leads the candidate. You may be able to lead the examiner, but there is a fine distinction between leading to things you know about and leading to the edge of a bottomless pit which you may be pushed into. Unless you are a very good candidate it is probably better to let the examiner do the leading and try and steer away from pits. Remember that questions often follow on from the previous answer so it is foolish to volunteer that you would estimate the shunt from the shunt equation if you do not know the shunt equation. Untruths are usually obvious as the following exchange shows. "What was the last anaesthetic you gave?" "D & C" "What about the one before that?" "D & C" "Don't you do any other procedures?" "I only do D&C's" Even if this were true, such a candidate would be unlikely to impress the examiners.

Equipment

There are lots of pieces of equipment around as a starting point for discussion e.g. spinal needles, ventimasks, various tubes, anaesthetic machines. If you do not know its name at least describe what it is for. Physics of equipment is asked: it is surprising how many people do not know the pressures at various points in an anaesthetic machine. Do not be surprised if you are asked to draw diagrams to illustrate points.

Long silences

You are not scoring any points when silent. Many examiners think of answers and then design questions to get that answer from the candidate. You may go round and round in circles without seeing what point is being sought. In these circumstances it is probably best to say you do not see what he is getting at, in the hope of moving on to something you do know about.

The Clinical Oral

In this part of the exam candidates are given 10 minutes on their own to study clinical material (there are no actual patients). This usually consists of history, examination findings and results of, for example, chest X-ray, ECG, pulmonary function tests, blood gases, biochemistry etc. Paper and pencil are provided for making notes while you study this. You then have 20-25 minutes with a pair of examiners who discuss the case and its anaesthetic implications with you. To ensure uniformity each batch of candidates studies the same material and the examiners have a series of guided questions which they may or may not stick to. If discussion of the main case does not fill the 25 minutes, there may be a supplementary topic introduced, again the same for each batch of candidates.

In the following section you are given case histories and results to study followed by questions. The best way to use it is to get a colleague to ask the questions and not to look at the answers until you have had a reasonable discussion of the problems raised. Most of the cases have a number of different problems to think about some are 'single problem' cases such as might be asked as a supplementary.

CASE HISTORY 1

A 51 year old advertising executive presents for extraction of his wisdom teeth.

History
He has not attended his doctor for many years and is on no medication.

Examination and Investigations
On admission to the ward his blood pressure is found to be 170/110 and he weighs 80 kg. A chest X-ray (Fig 1) and ECG (Fig 2) are performed.

Anaesthesia
After premedication with papaveretum 20 mg and hyoscine 0.4 mg anaesthesia is induced with thiopentone, the nasal mucosa sprayed with cocaine 10% 2 ml, and a nasotracheal tube is passed with the patient breathing spontaneously nitrous oxide, oxygen and halothane with 7% CO_2 to induce hyperventilation. A throat pack is inserted and the patient breathes N_2O 4 l/min:O_2 2 l/min, halothane 2% via a Bain circuit. During extraction of the teeth his BP rises to 200/115 and his ECG changes as shown (Fig 3).

Questions

1. Comment on his blood pressure on admission. How would you check on this reading?

2. Comment on the chest X-ray and ECG.

3. What should have been done before this patient was anaesthetised?

4. Was the method of induction appropriate for this patient?

5. What fresh gas flow would you have used for maintenance?

6. Comment on the operative ECG.

7. List possible causes for the rising BP and ECG abnormality.

CASE HISTORY 2

History
A 63 year old diabetic lady who lives alone is admitted to hospital with a history of being confused for two days, vomiting for 3 hours and pain in the right leg. Her diabetes is normally controlled on diet and chlorpropamide 250 mg daily. She also has angina for which she takes propranolol 40 mg tds and sublingual glyceryl trinitrate when required.

Examination
Her right foot is found to be gangrenous and a below knee amputation is proposed. She is barely conscious with a pulse of 113, BP 95/65 and weight 58 kg.

Investigations on admission are as follows:

WBC	11.7	x10^9/l	Plasma sodium	152	mmol/l
RBC	5.19	x10^{12}/l	potassium	5.3	mmol/l
Hb	15.1	g/dl	chloride	119	mmol/l
Hct	0.48		urea	25	mmol/l
MCV	92	fl	Serum albumin	57	g/l
MCH	29.1	Pg	Blood glucose	34.3	mmol/l
MCHC	31.4	g/dl	Urine glucose	2%	
			Urine ketones	neg	

Arterial blood gases breathing air:

pH	7.34
PCO$_2$	4.93 kPa (37 mmHg)
PO$_2$	10.9 kPa (81 mmHg)
HCO$_3$	19.8 mmol/l
TCO$_2$	20.8 mmol/l
BE	−5.1 mmol/l
SBC	18.8 mmol/l

Questions

1. Comment on the investigations and describe her metabolic state.

2. Estimate a) the plasma osmolality
          b) the change in her extracellular fluid volume.

3. How soon after admission should surgery go ahead?

4. How would you manage this patient before and during anaesthesia?

5. Briefly describe how you would manage the diabetes of this patient had she come in well controlled for elective minor surgery.

CASE HISTORY 3

An obese man aged 40 needs surgery for repair of an inguinal hernia.

History
He has always been obese. He has pains in the chest after meals and on severe exertion (which is rare for him).

Examination
Height 170 cm. Weight 100 kg.
Pulse 65/min. BP 150/90. No added heart sounds.

Investigations

Chest X-ray (Fig 4)
ECG (Fig 5)

Na	138 mmol/l	Bilirubin	9 mmol/l
K	4.3 mmol/l	Albumin	42 g/l
Cl	102 mmol/l	AST	24 iu/l
Urea	4.4 mmol/l	Alk phos	150 iu/l

Questions

1. Comment on the preoperative investigations.

2. Would you like any further investigations?

3. How much is he over his ideal weight?

4. List the main problems of the obese undergoing surgery.

5. What would be the major risk of giving this patient a general anaesthetic?

6. How could one anaesthetise this patient?

CASE HISTORY 4

History
A 69 year old female is scheduled for repair of a large incisional hernia, which has developed following a sigmoid colectomy for diverticulitis 2 years ago and closure of colostomy one year ago.

She gives an 8 year history of asthma and is also a mild hypertensive. She is on the following drugs:

Salbutamol and beclomethasone (Becotide) inhalers, 2 puffs up to 5 times daily, Moduretic 2 tablets daily, theophylline 400 mg nocte, prednisolone 7.5 mg mane. Nitrazepam, lorazepam, Normacol and Isogel were also in her collection of tablets.

Examination
Pulse 90/min. Blood pressure 140/90. Resps 16/min.

Respiratory function tests

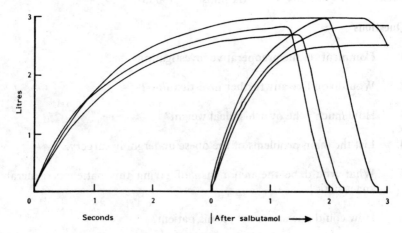

Vitalograph (3 attempts) before and after salbutamol

		% Predicted	after salbutamol
Peak expiratory flow rate	250 l/min	66%	345
FEV$_1$	1.7 l	61%	2.4
VC	3.0 l	80%	3.0
FEV$_1$/VC	56%		

Blood gases (breathing air) taken by the house surgeon from a femoral stab were:

pH	7.35		
PCO$_2$	6.13	kPa	(46 mmHg)
PO$_2$	5.60	kPa	(42 mmHg)
HCO$_3$	26.0	mmol/l	
TCO$_2$	27.3	mmol/l	
BE	+0.5	mmol/l	
SBC	25.1	mmol/l	

When repeated by the anaesthetist from a radial artery stab they were:

pH	7.42		
PCO$_2$	5.07	kPa	(38 mmHg)
PO$_2$	10.7	kPa	(80 mmHg)
HCO$_2$	24.4	mmol/l	
TCO$_2$	25.5	mmol/l	
BE	0	mmol/l	
SBC	24.5	mmol/l	

Questions

1. How do you interpret the pulmonary function tests?

2. How do you interpret the blood gases?

3. Would you require any further investigations?

4. How would you anaesthetise this patient?

5. What premedication would you choose?

CASE HISTORY 5

A 79 year old man weighing 63 kg is to undergo transurethral resection of his prostate. He was admitted with acute retention 2 days previously when he was catheterised. At that time his electrolytes were:

Na	138	mmol/l
K	4.9	mmol/l
Cl	104	mmol/l
Urea	8.2	mmol/l

On the morning of the operation they are:

Na	142	mmol/l
K	4.5	mmol/l
Cl	102	mmol/l
Urea	5.8	mmol/l

His ECG is shown (Fig 7)

After premedication with oral diazepam 5 mg he is given a spinal anaesthetic with heavy bupivacaine 2 ml which gives satisfactory anaesthesia up to T8. Transurethral resection is performed by the surgical registrar using glycine 1.5% as the irrigating solution. The operation proves to be difficult: 25 g of prostrate are resected, there is troublesome bleeding and the procedure takes 1 1/2 hours. Towards the end the patient becomes confused and disorientated and becomes even more confused and dyspoeic in recovery. His anaesthetic record is shown. (Fig 8)

Electrolytes taken in recovery are:

Na	118	mmol/l
K	3.5	mmol/l
Cl	85	mmol/l
Urea	3.5	mmol/l

His haematocrit is 32%

Arterial blood gases (breathing O_2 4 l/min by MC mask)

pH	7.45	
PCO_2	4.13	kPa (31 mmHg)
PO_2	8.0	kPa (60 mmHg)
HCO_3	21.5	mmol/l
TCO_2	22.5	mmol/l
BE	−2.0	mmol/l
SBC	22.5	mmol/l

Questions

1. Comment on the two sets of preoperative electrolytes.

2. What does his ECG show?

3. Are any special precautions necessary?

4. How do you interpret the changes in systolic BP shown on the anaesthetic record.

5. Why is the patient becoming confused at the end?

6. What would you expect to find on examining the patient's respiratory and cardiovascular systems in recovery? What does the chest X-ray (Fig 9) show?

7. Where should he go from the recovery room? What treatment needs to be started?

CASE HISTORY 6

A 40 year old accountant is admitted to Casualty with severe abdominal pain of sudden onset. The surgeons want to perform a laparotomy within the hour.

History
He has a long history of epigastric pain treated with cimetidine. He has had no previous operations. His brother had to spend some time in an Intensive Care Unit after a straightforward appendicitis.

Examination
Anxious
Pulse 110/min. BP 120/80. Respirations 16/min.
Board-like rigidity of the abdomen. No bowel sounds.

Investigations

Chest X-ray (Fig 10)

WBC	5.2	x 10^9/l
RBC	4.14	x 10^{12}/l
Hb	8.7	g/dl
Hct	0.31	
MCV	75	fl
MCH	21	pg
MCHC	28	g/dl

ECG taken at his last outpatient visit is available (Fig 11).

Questions

1. Comment on the chest X-ray.

2. What is the probable diagnosis?

3. Comment on the blood count and ECG.

4. What might the brother's problem have been? List the possibilities.

5. What further questions would you ask about the brother?

6. How might the answers modify your choice of drugs in this case?

7. Would you be prepared to anaesthetise the patient within an hour?

CASE HISTORY 7

A 39 year old lady is scheduled for laparotomy.

History
Lower abdominal swelling noticed over the last few weeks. No previous operations. Otherwise fit, jogs 2 miles every day.

Examination
Weight 50 kg. BP 130/80. Pulse 68/min. No abnormal findings. Chest X-ray shown (Fig 12).

Anaesthesia and Operation
Premedication: pethidine 75 mg, atropine 0.6 mg. Thiopentone 375 mg, fentanyl 100 µg, suxamethonium 100 mg. Following intubation, pancuronium 7 mg, fentanyl 100 µg, are given and she is ventilated with nitrous oxide 5 l/min oxygen 3 l/min and halothane 0.5% via a Manley ventilator, of the minute volume divider type. A simple ovarian cyst is removed and the procedure takes 30 minutes. At the end the patient will not breathe spontaneously despite neostigmine 2.5 mg and glycopyrrolate 0.6 mg.

Questions

1.   Comment on the chest X-ray.

2.   What are the possible causes of the patient's apnoea?

3.   How would you distinguish between them?

4.   How can they be treated?

CASE HISTORY 8

A 53 year old patient (photographed postoperatively in figures 13 and 14) presents for cataract extraction under general anaesthesia. He has not had an anaesthetic before, is otherwise fit and weighed 60 kg. He is pre-medicated with papaveretum 15 mg and hyoscine 0.3 mg, induced with thiopentone and paralysed with atracurium 35 mg. On direct laryngoscopy the junior anaesthetist is able to see the tip of the epiglottis but not the cords and is unable to intubate the trachea. It is easy to ventilate by mask but after further attempts at intubation a tear in the pharyngeal mucosa is noted. The procedure is abandoned at this stage. A postoperative neck X-ray is shown in Fig 15.

Questions

1. Would you have anticipated difficulty in intubating this patient?

2. What preoperative features would lead you to expect a difficult intubation?

3. As a junior anaesthetist what would you have done having found yourself unable to intubate?

4. What are the alternative methods of proceeding with the patient at this stage?

5. How and when would you reverse the muscle relaxation? What would you use to assess this?

6. What is shown on the X-ray (Fig 15).

7. If it is essential to intubate what techniques are available for the difficult intubation?

CASE HISTORY 9

A 35 year old man with an enlarged thyroid is to have it removed surgically.

History
Weight has been constant at 58 kg. Past history of hernia repair three years ago. He has been taking Lugol's iodine for 10 days.

Examination
Diffusely enlarged thyroid. No eye signs. Pulse regular 80/min. BP 130/80.

Investigations

Chest X-ray (Fig 16)

						Normal
Na	142	mmol/l	Thyroxine T$_4$	128	nmol/l	(60-140)
K	3.8	mmol/l	T$_3$	2.4	nmol/l	(1-3.5)
Ca	2.34	mmol/l	TSH	3.0	mU/l	($\approx$5)
Phosphate	1.3	mmol/l				
Albumin	43	g/l				

After premedication with pethidine 50 mg and atropine 0.6 mg IM one hour preoperatively, he is anaesthetised with methohexitone 60 mg, alcuronium 15 mg, pethidine 15 mg and ventilated via an oral endotracheal tube and a Manley ventilator using N$_2$O 4 l/min, O$_2$ 2 l/min and enflurane 0.4% (see chart Fig 17). Surgical removal of the goitre is difficult and damage to the right recurrent laryngeal nerve is suspected. On the first postoperative day clinical chemistry results are:

Na	139	mmol/l
K	4.0	mmol/l
Ca	2.04	mmol/l
Phosphate	1.62	mmol/l
Albumin	39	g/l

Questions

1. Are the history and investigations consistent with a diagnosis of thyrotoxicosis?

2. What are the abnormalities of thyroid function tests in

   a) hyperthyroidism
   b) hypothyroidism.

3. What is the effect of Lugol's iodine?

4. Comment on the X-ray (Fig 16).

5. What sort of endotracheal tube would you choose?

6. At the point where the anaesthetic record is stopped, what do you think might be happening?

7. What might be seen at laryngoscopy after extubation?

8. What do the tests on the first postoperative day suggest? What signs might be present? What immediate treatment needs to be given?

CASE HISTORY 10

A 22 year old African man is knocked down by a bus and brought unconscious to Casualty where he is intubated. On examination he is unconscious, but responds to painful stimuli in a purposeful manner. Pupils are equal and reacting. There are no localising neurological signs. He also has a Colle's fracture which the orthopaedic surgeons wish to reduce under anaesthesia.

Investigations
Skull X-ray (Figs 18 and 19)
Haemoglobin 12.8 g/l
Sickledex test: positive

Questions

1. Comment on the skull X-rays.

2. What does the Sickledex result tell you?

3. What further tests would you like?

4. What anaesthesia would you choose for the Colle's fracture reduction?

CASE HISTORY 11

A 47 year old Indian man is to have highly selective vagotomy for duodenal ulceration. He speaks no English and details of his past medical history are difficult to elicit, but he was admitted to another hospital 6 weeks ago with pain of some kind and kept in for 10 days. His preoperative ECG is shown (Fig 20).

Questions

1. Comment on the ECG.

2. What does it show?

3. Is he fit for anaesthesia?

4. What are the risks of anaesthesia and surgery in this patient?

CASE HISTORY 12

A patient arrives back in the Intensive Care Unit for elective ventilation following major surgery. On arrival in the unit at 18.15 his arterial blood gases being ventilated with 40% oxygen were:

pH	7.36	
PCO_2	5.5	kPa (41 mmHg)
PO_2	6.7	kPa (50 mmHg)
HCO_3	23.0	mmol/l
TCO_2	24.4	mmol/l
BE	−2.0	mmol/l
SBC	22.3	mmol/l

A portable chest X-ray taken at 18.20 is shown in Fig 21. Subsequent X-rays at 19.00 (Fig 22) and midnight (Fig 23) are also provided.

Questions

1. What is the difference between a portable AP and the usual PA chest X-ray?

2. How do you interpret the blood gases and chest X-ray (Fig 21) taken on arrival in ITU?

3. Comment on the next chest film (19.00 Fig 22). What has been done since the first film. Would you expect an improvement in blood gases?

4. What should be done next?

5. Comment on the final (midnight) X-ray (Fig 23).

CASE HISTORY 13

A 74 year old lady was admitted to the surgical wards for limited resection of a breast lump. She complained of occasional dizzy spells. On examination her pulse was regular, 46 per minute; BP 140/85; JVP 0; and apart from the breast lump, there were no other abnormal findings. Her ECG is shown (Fig 24).

Questions

1. What does the ECG show?

2. Could this explain her dizziness?

3. How can she be treated?

4. Should this be done before anaesthesia?

Fig 1. Case 1.

Fig 2. Case 1.

Fig 3. Case 1.

67

Fig 4. Case 3.

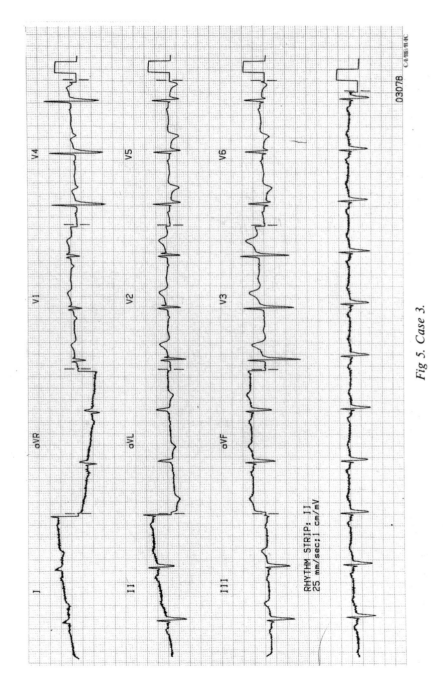

Fig 5. Case 3.

69

Fig 6. Case 3.

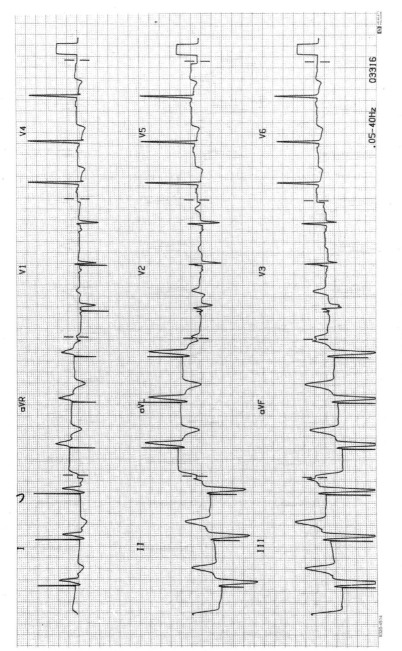

Fig 7. Case 5.

71

Fig 8. Case 5.

Fig 9. Case 5.

Fig 10. Case 6.

Fig 11. Case 6.

Fig 12. Case 7.

Fig 13. Case 8.

Fig 14. Case 8.

Fig 15. Case 8.

Fig 16. Case 9.

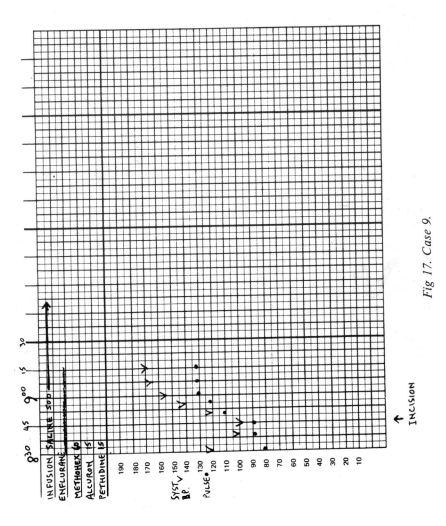

Fig 17. Case 9.

81

Fig 18. Case 10.

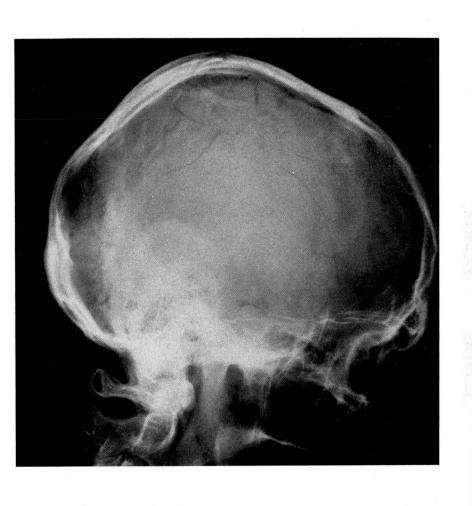

Fig 19. Case 10.

Fig 20. Case 11.

Fig 21. Case 12.

Fig 22. Case 12. 19.00 hrs.

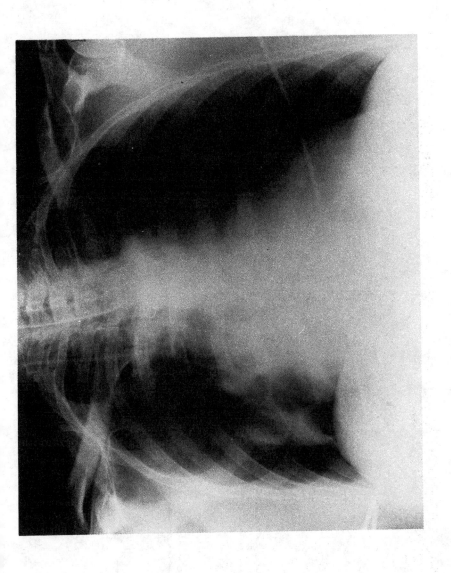

Fig 23. Case 12. midnight.

Fig 24. Case 13.

ANSWERS AND EXPLANATIONS FOR MCQ PAPERS

ANSWERS TO MCQ PRACTICE EXAM 1

The correct answer options are given against each question number.

1. **A C D E**
   True anaphylactic allergy to thiopentone does occur and is characterised by periorbital oedema, urticarial rash, marked hypotension and bronchospasm. The mechanism is a type 1 hypersensitivity, mediated by IgE antibodies, which are consumed during the reaction.

2. **A C E**
   Plasma protein solutions (Plasma Protein Fraction, or Human Albumin Solution) are stored at room temperature but should be kept away from light. They are prepared from fractionation of large pools of donor plasma, but the final product is sterilized by pasteurization at 60°C for 10 hours and there is said to be no risk of transmitting viruses. They contain about 4.5 g/dl of protein, principally as albumin and 145 mmol/l of sodium as the solution is reconstituted in saline. Fresh frozen plasma is required to treat disseminated intravascular coagulation as it is the only solution to retain clotting factors.

3. **D**
   Thrombosis following an intravenous injection can follow the administration of thiopentone, etomidate, propofol and methohexitone but it is uncommon, even with etomidate, propofol and methohexitone which can cause pain on injection. Diazepam in propylene glycol is a well recognised cause of thrombophlebitis and thrombosis.

4. **A B C D E**
   Intravascular administration of local anaesthetic is a risk with any local block where the needle is close to blood vessels, the subclavian artery lies on the first rib immediately in front of the brachial plexus, careful aspiration prior to injection is essential. Pneumothorax is a well recognised risk and is said to have an incidence of 0.5 to 6%. If solution is injected outside the sheath of the plexus it may ascend in the tissue planes to block other nerves. The phrenic is most often involved and the diaphragm on that side will be paralysed, the risk of this and of pneumothorax leads to a general recommendation

that bilateral blocks are best avoided. The vagus, recurrent laryngeal, and sympathetic nerves can also be blocked and the latter will result in Horner's syndrome.

5. **A B C**

Trauma and anxiety give rise to increased sympathetic tone which delays gastric emptying. Morphine causes an increase in tone in the antral portion of the stomach, this reduces gastric emptying and can prevent passage into the first part of the duodenum for up to 12 hours. Metoclopramide increases gastric emptying and ranitidine reduces acid secretion without any action on emptying time.

6. **C D E**

The approximate composition of soda lime is about 90% calcium hydroxide, 5% sodium hydroxide and 1% potassium hydroxide with the addition of silicates to prevent powdering. The moisture content is 14–19% and this is essential for effective carbon dioxide absorption. Calcium carbonate is formed as the hydroxides combine with carbon dioxide in the presence of water. The size and shape of the granules is important to ensure an adequate surface area for absorption and to minimise resistance to respiration, in a properly packed canister half the volume should be space between the granules. Heat is produced by the chemical reaction that takes place but modern soda limes such as Durasorb, become much less hot than the older types. Nitrous oxide is unaffected by soda lime.

7. **A**

50 mg of suxamethonium is a modest dose for an adult (normal dose 1 mg/kg) and the absence of breathing for 1 hour, raises the suspicion of the patient having an abnormal gene for cholinesterase. Although plasma cholinesterases can be provided by an infusion of fresh, or fresh frozen plasma, stored blood contains no cholinesterases. Malignant hyperpyrexia is characterised by rigidity, hyperpyrexia, cardiac arrhythmias and must be treated promptly. Suxamethonium raises the plasma potassium and intravenous neostigmine reverses non-depolarising block but can intensify a depolarising block, if suxamethonium cannot be metabolised then this will only create further problems.

8. **D**

MCQ questions involving clinical situations require a cautious approach as in reality such situations are rarely clearly defined. First analyse the data provided, the PCO_2 is raised and the cardiovascular changes described could be secondary to this. There is arterial hypoxaemia. A simple serum bicarbonate will be influenced by the PCO_2 unlike a standard bicarbonate value, but a result at the upper end of the normal range rules out a metabolic acidosis. Septicaemia is characterised by a fall in BP. Transfusion initially will lead to a rise in the CVP and cardiovascular parameters may improve, but over-transfusion overloads the right and left sides of the heart and the BP falls. Segmental pulmonary collapse results in increased intrapulmonary shunting and arterial hypoxaemia, but if ventilation is maintained in the rest of the lung, CO_2 elimination is unchanged and the arterial PCO_2 does not rise. The changes described can occur with under-ventilation in the postoperative period resulting in hypercarbia and hypoxaemia.

9. **A B C**
In overdose local anaesthetic drugs are depressant to the CVS and CNS. Hypotension and cardiovascular collapse may occur but in the CNS stimulation precedes depression, probably as a result of inhibitory centres being blocked first. Restlessness with involuntary movements and convulsions may be seen before loss of consciousness and respiratory depression.

10. **B D E**
Warming blood reduces the incidence of arrhythmias due to hypothermia, acidosis and hyperkalaemia. Blood should not be left out of the refrigerator for long periods to re-warm as this increases the risk of infection but the use of standard blood warmers is satisfactory. Increasing the temperature of blood shifts the oxygen dissociation curve to the right. Gases are more soluble in liquids at lower temperatures (cold lager is less fizzy), so that in blood as the temperature rises less is dissolved and the partial pressure rises, this is more marked with a soluble gas such as CO_2 than with a less soluble one, such as O_2. Thus for CO_2: PCO_2 at 20°C=15 mmHg PCO_2 at 37°C=34.8 mmHg.

11. **A C E**
Aminophylline, by blocking the enzyme phosphodiestersase, allows the build up of cyclic AMP which leads to relaxation of bronchial smooth muscle. Salbutamol selectively stimulates the β_2-receptors in the lung and they in turn activate adenyl cyclase which increases cyclic AMP producing the same effect as above. Halothane at deeper levels of anaesthesia, reduces bronchomotor tone and can be helpful in overcoming bronchospasm. Propranolol must not be given to asthmatics as it blocks the β_2-receptors in the lung.

12. **B D**

Space blankets primarily minimise radiant heat loss from the surface of the body but by covering the patient they also reduce loss by convection. Normally anaesthetic gases are dry and as they are humidified in the airway liquid water turns to vapour, this requires latent heat and leads to cooling of the surrounding tissues, humidifying the inspired gases prevents this happening. With a patient at 37°C and the theatre at 20°C there will be considerable cooling, the theatre temperature needs to be raised to around 26°C to 28°C if a serious attempt is being made to reduce heat loss, as for instance in paediatric surgery. Phenothiazines induce peripheral vasodilatation and have been used to promote surface cooling during induced hypothermia, the route by which fluids are given is not relevant.

13. **C E**

An endotracheal tube that is too long is more likely to pass into the right main bronchus than the left as the latter branches at a more acute angle. Occlusion of the secondary bronchus to the right upper lobe which branches off to the right 2.5 cm below the carina, will eventually cause collapse of the right upper lobe but not within 5 minutes. Collapse of the left lung increases intrapulmonary shunting and results in a reduction of the uptake of less soluble gases such as oxygen leading to hypoxaemia but not hypotension. Likewise the uptake of relatively insoluble anaesthetic gases or volatile agents will be reduced. By comparison, maintaining the ventilation allows a soluble gas such as CO_2 to be effectively eliminated.

14. **A B E**

Depolarising muscle relaxants such as suxamethonium and decamethonium cause depolarisation of the motor end-plate of the same kind as that produced by acetylcholine, but the block persists. Excessive dosage with neostigmine and edrophonium can lead to such a build up of acetylcholine, due to inhibition of cholinesterase a depolarising block results. It is therefore recommended that not more than 5 mg of neostigmine be given to reverse non-depolarising muscle relaxants. Atracurium and vecuronium are non-depolarising muscle relaxants.

15. **A B E**

In the obese the functional residual capacity falls and the closing capacity encroaches into it so as to lie within the range of the tidal volume, this leads to increased ventilation-perfusion mismatch and arterial hypoxaemia. The Pickwickian syndrome in which airway problems, particularly during sleep, lead to hypoventilation and hypercarbia can also occur but is less common than hypoxaemia. Intubation is often technically difficult, a laryngoscope with a long blade and a stilette for the endotracheal tube should be available. Although the assessment of drug dosage in the obese may be more difficult, in relating their lean body mass and fat to the drug being used, there is no specific increase in sensitivity in these patients to either thiopentone or the non-depolarising muscle relaxants.

16.   D

The Association of Anaesthetists has published a booklet 'Checklist for Anaesthetic Machines' (available from the Association of Anaesthetists of Great Britain and Ireland, 9 Bedford Square, London WC1B 3RA). This checklist is a recommended procedure based on the use of an oxygen analyser.

The check commences with the machine disconnected from all pipeline supplies and all vaporisers turned to 'off'. A series of manoeuvres are then performed to ensure that the correct gas flows through the corresponding flowmeter. The basis of which is that the flowmeters are opened and the gas supply, either from the cylinders or the pipeline, is sequentially connected up and the flowmeters observed to ensure that only the oxygen flowmeter is influenced by connection to an oxygen supply. The incorporation of an oxygen analyser into the procedure adds security to these exercises.

Modern oxygen alarms sound an audible warning activated by falling oxygen pressure alone, but the diversion of the nitrous oxide supply through the whistle prolongs this audible warning. On modern anaesthetic machines the vaporisers are interlocked preventing the operator from turning on more than one vaporiser at a time. In the recommendations checking of the vaporiser commences with it turned off and with a flow rate of oxygen of 6–8 litres per minute the gas outlet is occluded, there should be no leak from the vaporiser fitments and the flowmeter bobbin should dip. This test is then repeated with the vaporiser in the on position to ensure no leaks from the filling port.

A pressure relief valve set at 30 kPa is fitted on the machine, this is intended to protect the machine not the patient and should open when the gas outlet is occluded. Bodock seals are the small ring seals between the cylinder outlet and the pin index head, they are replaced only when they become worn and cause leaks. With pipeline supplies, cylinders are now replaced infrequently and the seals may last for many weeks.

17. **B D E**

A rise in pulse rate and sweating are signs of light or inadequate depth of anaesthesia, this is not directly related to the level of muscle relaxation. When paralysis wears off and muscle tone returns there may be swallowing and increase in tone in the respiratory muscles reducing chest compliance and leading to an increase in inflation pressure with a volume cycled ventilator. The incidence of hiccup is said to be greater when muscle relaxants are used, it is often difficult to abolish requiring deep levels of anaesthesia or complete muscle paralysis.

18. **A C E**

Enflurane causes more respiratory depression than halothane. Both agents are depressant to the myocardium but at equal MAC enflurane is more so and causes a greater fall in cardiac output than halothane. Cardiac arrhythmias are uncommon with enflurane and there is less sensitisation of the myocardium to catecholamines than occurs with halothane, with adrenaline infiltration up to three times more may safely be given. More halothane is metabolised than enflurane but whereas halothane produces negligible amounts of inorganic fluoride, enflurane does produce it although the levels are not high enough to cause renal problems. Boiling points – halothane 50°C, enflurane 56°C.

19. **E**

Intravenous regional anaesthesia was described by Bier in 1908 but he used procaine, lignocaine not being introduced until 1948. A vein on the dorsum of the hand should be chosen since if the cannula is placed proximally in a large vein with valves distally, local anaesthetic may be forced under the cuff even if it is correctly inflated to 100 mmHg above systolic pressure. Following a number of fatalities with the technique (due to various errors) bupivacaine is no longer recommended. Prilocaine 0.5% plain solution, at a dose of 3 mg/kg is the drug of choice being less likely to cause CNS toxicity than lignocaine which is also used. Sickle cell disease, both homozygous and heterozygous is an absolute contraindication to the technique because of the use of a tourniquet.

20. **A B**

Thiopentone causes a reduction of the cardiac output by depression of myocardial contractility and peripheral vasodilatation. Severe hypotension may occur if too much is given or if the patient cannot compensate for the CVS changes, this is most likely to occur in constrictive pericarditis and tamponade, tight valvular stenosis, complete heart block, hypovolaemia and adrenocortical insufficiency. Respiratory depression with thiopentone results from depression of the respiratory centre, it depends on the dose, speed of injection and the presence of other central depressants such as opiates. Thiopentone lowers the intracranial pressure, is not toxic to the liver and it is anticonvulsant.

21. **B D**

Dantrolene is a skeletal muscle relaxant and it acts not at the neuromuscular junction but directly on the sarcoplasmic reticulum, uncoupling the excitation-contraction sequence by reducing calcium release. It is the specific agent for the acute treatment of malignant hyperpyrexia but can also be given prophylactically in known susceptible subjects undergoing anaesthesia. Its muscle relaxant properties would cause it to potentiate myoneural block in normal subjects.

22. **A**

In flutter digoxin is used as it shortens the refractory period of the myocardial cells and tends to convert the flutter to fibrillation, if the digoxin is then stopped the heart may revert to sinus rhythm. Digoxin is not otherwise of value in heart block, Stokes-Adams attacks or ventricular tachycardia. Nodal tachycardia is difficult to differentiate from other types of supraventricular tachycardia but digoxin is of no value in its treatment, and nodal tachycardia can in fact result from digoxin toxicity.

23. **A B C**

Dopamine has a biphasic action, at lower doses it is primarily a β-stimulant but at higher doses it exhibits an α-stimulant action. Infused at a dosage of 10 μg/kg/minute it is a β-stimulant, renal blood flow is increased by vasodilatation and stimulation of 'dopamine receptors' in the renal artery, this results in an increased urinary output and sodium output. Cardiac contractility is improved but without a rise in heart rate and the cardiac output is increased. Infused at a dosage of 20 μg/kg/minute or more, α-stimulation predominates and multiple ventricular extrasystoles and other dysrhythmias may occur. The peripheral resistance is reduced with lower doses and increased with higher doses.

24. **C E**

Isoprenaline and glucagon increase the blood glucose concentration by mobilising glycogen stored in the liver. Growth hormone is diabetogenic and as well as mobilising glycogen, it inhibits the uptake of glucose into some tissues. Metformin is a biguanide and glibenclamide is a sulphonylurea, both are used in the treatment of diabetes, the former increases peripheral utilisation of glucose and the latter augments insulin secretion, they are only effective when there is some residual pancreatic β-cell activity.

25. **A B D**
Atracurium is a bis-quaternary ammonium compound, the two halves of which are connected by an ester linkage. It is destroyed in vivo by a combination of the Hofmann elimination and ester hydrolysis. This makes it particularly suitable for use in anephric patients because elimination is independent of renal function. Laudanosine is one of the breakdown products. Although it has CNS effects in animals this is not a problem in clinical doses in man. Histamine may be released but the effects are local rather than systemic. In a large post-marketing surveillance study broncho-spasm was no more common with atracurium than vecuronium. Atracurium precipitates with thiopentone solutions.

26. **A B**
Alfentanil produces direct depression of the medullary respiratory centre, as a result there is a shift to the right and a reduction in the slope of the carbon dioxide response curve. The half life of alfentanil is 1–3 hours and that of fentanyl is 2–7 hours. It has no effect on uterine muscle, causes minimal myocardial depression and is less potent than fentanyl, requiring a higher dosage to achieve an equivalent effect.

27. **B C D E**
Thiopentone is supplied mixed with anhydrous sodium carbonate as it is only soluble in alkaline solution, the pH of a 2.5% solution being 10.5. Chemically it is the sulphur analogue of pentobarbitone, the sulphur replacing oxygen and imparting a more rapid action and recovery. In the blood about 70% is normally bound to plasma proteins and in malnutrition and other conditions where plasma proteins are low, there will be more free drug increasing the patient's sensitivity. The blood pH also affects plasma binding, raising the pH as in hyperventilation, increases the unbound portion. Thiopentone has a pKa of 7.6 and in the plasma at a pH of 7.4 about 60% is present in the non-ionised form. The clinical effects of an induction dose of thiopentone cease as the drug is redistributed in the body mainly to fat, metabolism is slow. Although traces are excreted unchanged in the urine, the majority is broken down in the liver and excreted through the kidneys and gut. About 10–15% is destroyed each hour so that at the end of 24 hours almost 30% of the original dose may remain in the body.

28. A C D

Hyoscine differs from atropine in its peripheral actions, by having a more potent anti-muscarinic effect on the eye and the secretions of the gut, bronchial and sweat glands; whereas atropine has a more marked action on the smooth muscle of the bronchi and GI tract as well as the heart. Both drugs are anti-emetic but hyoscine is the more effective particularly in motion sickness, hence its use for the invasion troops on D-day. It is also the better anti-sialogogue. The central action of atropine is to stimulate and then depress in high dosage, whereas hyoscine is only sedative. However there are exceptions, the anti-Parkinsonian action of atropine in reducing tremor is purely depressant and in the elderly hyoscine sometimes causes excitement and restlessness.

29. A B

When a nerve stimulator is used, fade and post-tetanic facilitation are characteristics of non-depolarising muscle blockade. Acetylcholine can itself produce a depolarising block and neostigmine, by increasing its concentration at the neuromuscular junction, will tend to potentiate depolarising relaxants. The presence of d-tubocurarine limits the ability of suxamethonium to get to the receptors and thereby antagonises its action. Lowering body temperature potentiates the action of depolarising agents.

30. B E

Local anaesthetics act by blocking membrane depolarisation in excitable tissues in the body, placed in proximity to peripheral nerves they block the spread of the nerve impulse and if they reach the general circulation they affect in particular the brain and conductive tissues of the heart. They are either esters (cocaine, procaine, amethocaine) or amides (lignocaine, bupivacaine, prilocaine) and are detoxified in the liver. Methaemoglobinaemia is not seen with bupivacaine but is an occasional feature of the use of prilocaine. 2 mg/kg body weight is the generally recommended maximum dose in a 4 hour period, with or without adrenaline.

31. B D

Doxapram is a CNS stimulant, it produces its action on respiration via two mechanisms:
1. activation of carotid chemoreceptors;
2. stimulation of respiratory neurones in the medulla.

It increases whole body oxygen consumption and it can cause convulsions in doses slightly greater than the therapeutic dose. It is metabolised in the liver, but its short duration of action is due to redistribution.

32.　D E

In the CNS ketamine induces a rapid loss of consciousness and good analgesia but the unpleasant dreams and hallucinations that occur on emergence have limited its clinical use. It raises the BP, unlike most other general anaesthetics, and is therefore contraindicated in hypertensive patients. This action does give it a place as an induction agent in emergency anaesthesia of the shocked patient particularly in military or disaster situations. It is used in plastic surgery mainly for children and could be used with facial burns, the airway is usually well maintained but should always be carefully watched. Although ketamine does not relax the uterus, it does cross the placenta and fetal concentrations are equal to those in the mother. In addition the airway is not safe from aspiration, it is therefore not suitable for caesarean section even as an induction agent.

33.　A B C D E

Dirt on the bobbin and static electricity may cause the bobbin to stick to the glass tubing resulting in large inaccuracies. Rotameters are calibrated for an individual gas at sea level, changes in the gas or ambient pressure will lead to inaccuracy. Ventilators that exert back pressure such as the Manley will depress the level of the bobbin and errors of up to 7% may result.

34.　A B C D E

For flammable anaesthetics the concentration range of flammability in air is less than that in oxygen, e.g. diethyl ether 1.85–36.5% in air and 2.1–82% in oxygen. Ether will burn in air but only explode in oxygen. Nitrous oxide also supports combustion. Build up of static electricity is minimised by relative humidity $\simeq 50\%$, conductive flooring (0.1–10 Mohms) and the substitution of cotton for wool blankets etc.

35　A C

The transition from gas to liquid is in three stages, above the critical temperature it is a gas, between critical temperature and boiling point it is a vapour and below the boiling point it is a liquid. The critical temperature is therefore defined as the temperature above which a gas cannot be liquefied by pressure alone. In the case of oxygen the critical temperature is $-118.4°C$ and the boiling point is $-182.5°C$, when liquid oxygen is stored in Vacuum Insulated Evaporators (VIEs) for supply to the hospital pipeline it is at a temperature of $-165°C$. As this is below the critical temperature and at a pressure of 1200 kPa, it is liquid. Only below the boiling point would it be liquid at atmospheric pressure. For nitrous oxide the critical temperature is $36.5°C$.

36. **E**
Entonox cylinders are filled to the same pressure as oxygen cylinders which is 120 kPa x100 or 1950 lb/in². There should be no water vapour in a nitrous oxide cylinder and storage at low temperature is not a problem, unlike Entonox which should not be stored below −8°C.

37. **A E**
The problem with anatomy is relating a two-dimensional drawing to a three-dimensional reality, the epidural space is a particularly difficult example. The sacrococcygeal membrane closes off the lower end of the epidural space and is punctured by the needle in caudal block. The anterior longitudinal ligament lies in front of the vertebral bodies and is well away from the epidural space, it is the posterior longitudinal ligament at the back of the vertebral bodies which is in relation. The lamina lie posteriorly to the space and it is their anterior rather than posterior surfaces which bound the space. The interspinous ligament runs between the spines of the vertebrae and is well away. The nerve roots pass from the spinal canal through the dura to the intervertebral foramen and it is one of theories as to the mode of action of epidural block that the individual nerves are blocked at these so-called cuff areas, the intervertebral foramen therefore form a boundary of the epidural space.

38. **A B C D**
Anatomically the three cervical sympathetic ganglia are fused with the upper thoracic ganglion to form the stellate ganglion. When they are blocked the sympathetic supply to the head and neck is lost. This results in Horner's syndrome: miosis, enophthalmos and ptosis. In addition there is dilatation of the conjunctival vessels, lack of sweating of the face on the same side as the block and nasal congestion (Guttmann's sign).

39. **C E**
Carbon monoxide has an affinity for haemoglobin 210 greater than oxygen and carboxyhaemoglobin is only slowly eliminated even in the presence of high oxygen concentrations. There is no effect on the chemoreceptors. Heavy smokers may have up to 15% carboxyhaemoglobin, hence the importance of stopping smoking prior to anaesthesia. The presence of carboxyhaemoglobin shifts the oxygen dissociation curve to the left.

40.   B C
Bronchial calibre increases with sympathetic β-stimulation and decreases with parasympathetic stimulation. Histamine causes bronchoconstriction by direct action on H_1-receptors in bronchial smooth muscle. The calibre of the bronchi increases in inspiration and decreases during coughing.

41.   A C E
PO_2 falls progressively from:
   i)   inspired air to trachea because of saturation at 37°C with water vapour;
   ii) trachea to alveolus mainly because of the addition of CO_2;
   iii) alveolus to arterial blood [(A-a) PO_2 gradient] because of shunts and V/Q mismatching.
Everyone has a small anatomical shunt due to bronchial and thebesian vein drainage. Cyanosis is not caused by hypercarbia, although low O_2 saturation and high CO_2 often occur together, hypercarbia does not cause cyanosis and can occur with normal O_2 saturation if the FIO_2 is high.

42.   A D E
The normal $PaCO_2$ is 5.3 kPa (40 mmHg) and the mixed venous CO_2 is 6.1 kPa (46 mmHg). The majority of CO_2 is carried in blood in the form of bicarbonate ion which varies with the PCO_2. Low PIO_2 at altitude causes hyperventilation and lowering of $PaCO_2$. There is usually a small rise of $PaCO_2$ 0.4 kPa (3 mmHg) during sleep.

43.   A C D E
$PaCO_2$ falls by the 12th week of pregnancy to 4 kPa (30 mmHg) as a result of an increase in tidal volume without an increase in rate. Functional residual capacity is reduced from the 20th week.

44.   A D E
The systemic vascular resistance is about ten times higher than the pulmonary vascular resistance. Pregnancy, exercise and isoflurane all cause vasodilation and a fall in peripheral resistance. In vasovagal syncope excessive vagal tone causes bradycardia, and a fall in systemic resistance. Consciousness is lost due to the sudden fall in cardiac output.

45.   A B D
Cardiac output closely parallels oxygen consumption, it rises with increased myocardial contractility and with increased diastolic filling, as predicted by Starling's law. An increased afterload causes a rise in myocardial contractility to maintain cardiac output.

46. A C D
The SA and AV nodes consist of rhythmically discharging cells, each impulse is followed by a declining membrane potential which triggers the next impulse, the speed of decline determines the rate of discharge. Stimulation of the vagal fibres to the SA and AV node releases acetylcholine which slows the rate at which the membrane potential falls (repolarisation). The result is a decrease in heart rate and a prolongation of AV conduction.

47. None correct
The CSF is secreted by the choroid plexus in the lateral ventricles and passes through the 3rd and 4th ventricles to reach the surface of the brain. It is reabsorbed into the sagittal sinus by the arachnoid villi. It has a volume of about 125–135 ml and its pH and protein content are lower than the plasma, being 7·23 compared with 7·35 and 24 compared with 40 mg/100 ml, respectively. The glucose content in CSF is 2·5-4 mmol/l compared with 4-5 mmol/l in plasma.

48. B C
The cerebral circulation, like the coronary, has insignificant sympathetic vasoconstrictor innervation and is therefore spared in the vasoconstriction that follows haemorrhage. Increased discharge from the baroreceptors inhibits the vasomotor centre and lowers BP, in haemorrhage therefore, baroreceptor discharge decreases.

Fall in BP and vasoconstriction in the renal circulation result in a fall in glomerular filtration rate. Production of both ADH and aldosterone increases causing retention of sodium and water.

49. A
Changes in the arterial PCO_2 have a profound effect on the cerebral blood flow; at 8 kPa the rise would be about 50% above normal, whereas hyperventilation will lower the flow. A head down posture causes a rise in venous pressure and this decreases cerebral blood flow both by decreasing the effective perfusion pressure and by compressing the cerebral vessels. Autoregulation maintains a steady cerebral blood flow despite moderate changes in the BP. The effect of the PaO_2 is small, a PaO_2 of under 8 kPa (60 mmHg) will cause a slight rise in cerebral blood flow.

50. D E
Pressures in the chambers of the heart vary especially in the atria, but in general normal values are: RA mean 1–2 mmHg, RV 28/0 mmHg, LA mean 5 mmHg, LV 125/3 mmHg. There should be no pressure gradient across the pulmonary valve, RV and PA systolic pressures should be the same, if the PA is lower then stenosis is

present. Blood in the pulmonary artery is mixed venous blood having drained from all the tissues of the body including the heart, it has a saturation of 75%. Having traversed the pulmonary circulation it arrives in the LA fully saturated.

51. A B C E
Down's Syndrome (trisomy 21) is associated with atrial septal defects and an incidence of leukaemia three times greater than the normal. The nasal bridge is low, the mouth small, the tongue large. Webbing of the neck occurs in Turner's Syndrome.

52. A C D E
In gastro-intestinal obstruction, large volumes of fluid are lost from the ECF into the bowel lumen. In a severe case this may be as much as 10% of body weight. With prolonged vomiting there is loss of hydrogen and potassium ions leading to alkalosis and hypokalaemia which in turn may lead to cardiac arrhythmias. Epidural anaesthesia by paralysing sympathetic activity in the bowel, leaving parasympathetic contractions unopposed, can result in bowel rupture.

53. A B C D E
Angina pectoris, pain due to myocardial ischaemia, can result from any situation in which the coronary blood flow and the supply of oxygen are insufficient for the needs of the myocardium. Although coronary atheroma is the commonest cause, polyarteritis can also constrict the coronary vessels. Anaemia reduces the supply of oxygen to the coronary circulation and increases the cardiac output in order to satisfy the oxygen requirements of the tissues. Aortic stenosis and paroxysmal ventricular tachycardia both increase the work of the myocardium and may lead to angina. Angina pectoris is a recognised feature of myxoedema and results from the widespread degenerative vascular disease and hypertension which are often present in this condition.

54. A E
The absorption into the circulation of irrigating fluids used at TURPs is well recognised. There is dilutional hyponatraemia which can cause confusion, convulsions and coma, pulmonary oedema, acute left heart failure and cardiac arrest. Glycine 1.5% is isotonic which prevents haemolysis.

55. B D E
The prothrombin time is affected by deficiencies in the levels of factors II, VII, IX and X (all synthesised by the liver). Vitamin K, a fat soluble vitamin is necessary for the formation of prothrombin

(factor II). Its absorption is impaired in obstructive jaundice (but not haemolytic) and in steatorrhoea thus prolonging prothrombin time.

56. A C
Chronic deficiency of hormones of the adrenal cortex is Addison's disease and is associated with the loss of sodium from the body leading to a low serum sodium and low BP. The serum potassium rises. Abdominal striae are seen in Cushing's syndrome which is due to an excessive secretion of hormones from the adrenal cortex.

57. A B
Chronic bronchitis develops in response to the long continued action of various types of irritant, particularly cigarette smoke, on the bronchial mucosa. It is characterised by increased mucus secretion and mucosal oedema which tend to block the bronchioles and result in alveolar air trapping in expiration. This alveolar distension leads to an increase in residual volume. The FEV_1/FVC ratio falls and in severe cases may be as low as 30% (normal 70%). Although some patients die within a few years, others survive for many years with a gradually diminishing respiratory reserve.

58. A C D
Bed rest, neoplastic disease and obesity all favour the formation of deep venous thrombosis. Epidural anaesthesia has been shown in a number of studies to decrease the incidence although the reason for this is not clear.

59. D E
Iron deficiency anaemia is microcytic (reduced MCV) and hypochromic (reduced MCHC) and target cells are present. 2,3 diphosphoglycerate (2,3-DPG) levels are increased which shifts the haemoglobin dissociation curve to the right making more oxygen available for unloading at low PO_2 in the tissues. Stored blood gradually loses its 2,3-DPG thus shifting the curve to the left which impedes oxygen release in the tissues. The 2,3-DPG levels are restored within a few hours of transfusion. Alkalosis also shifts the curve to the left with the same effect. The oxygen tension (PO_2) is unaffected although the total oxygen content is reduced.

60. B D
Emphysema and chronic bronchitis represent two extremes of a clinical spectrum and many patients have features of both. However there are patients who fall into one of the two traditional categories of pink puffer or blue bloater. Pink puffers are typically dyspnoeic

with hyperinflation but usually maintain a normal arterial PCO_2 and a reasonable PO_2. In contrast, blue bloaters have a raised arterial PCO_2 and a lower PO_2 probably as a result of reduced sensitivity of the respiratory centre to CO_2 as well as the increased work of breathing. As a result of chronic respiratory acidosis they develop a compensatory metabolic alkalosis with a raised standard bicarbonate. They also have polycythaemia because of chronic hypoxaemia. Transfer factor is lower in the emphysematous patient because of the loss of alveolar walls resulting in less area for the diffusion of carbon monoxide.

ANSWERS TO MCQ PRACTICE EXAM 2

1. **A B D E**
Retention of urine and itching are well recognised complications of epidural opiates. Morphine may cause nausea and vomiting when given by this route, just as it can when given systemically. Respiratory depression is the most worrying potential complication of this technique, it is not common but tends to occur earlier with lipophylic narcotics such as fentanyl and methadone than with those having a low lipid solubility such as pethidine and morphine.

2. **A D E**
Convulsions can occur with deep ether anaesthesia both intra-operatively and postoperatively. Hypoxia may also be the cause of convulsions particularly in the postoperative period. Local anaesthetic drugs in overdose can lead to convulsions by depression of the inhibitory centres in the brain. Neither fasiculations following suxamethonium nor the myoclonus which is often seen after halothane anaesthesia and may be incorrectly referred to as shivering, have their origin in the CNS.

3. **A B C**
In Mapleson's classification, the Magill and the Lack circuits are type A, the latter being a coaxial version. The effort required to open the expiratory valve of the Magill circuit precludes its use in small children but it is suitable for those weighing more than 20 kg (generally over the age of 5). In spontaneously breathing patients it has been shown that the fresh gas flow can be reduced to less than the minute volume without rebreathing and hypercarbia occurring. In this situation there will be rebreathing of gas that has been in the anatomical dead space but as this has not been involved in gas exchange, it will be the same as fresh gas. Under ideal conditions

the fresh gas flow can be reduced to alveolar ventilation (normally about 70% of minute volume) without rebreathing taking place and the arterial PCO_2 rising. When used for IPPV the expiratory valve must be partially closed and rebreathing will occur even at high fresh gas flows; although this may be permissible for short periods when it is not intended to lower the PCO_2, as for instance whilst waiting for the effects of suxamethonium to wear off, it is not satisfactory for longer periods of IPPV.

4.   C E

Thiopentone at a concentration of 2.5% can cause damage on injection into arteries. The incidence and severity of the sequelae are reduced with this concentration, as compared with the 5% solution which was used at one time, but gangrene can occur even with 2.5%. The pain is due to arterial spasm, as a result of release of noradrenaline from the vessel walls. Stellate ganglion block produces paresis of the sympathetic supply to the arm and may reduce this spasm. Damage may result from injection into an artery at any site, and the onset of unconsciousness will be delayed.

5.   A E

Clinical assessment of recovery following neuromuscular block is never as reliable as the use of a nerve stimulator which should be part of the regular routine of using relaxants. In states of partial paralysis it is difficult to quantitate the degree of block with clinical signs. The ability to sustain a head lift for 5 seconds is probably the generally most useful test and it correlates well with the train-of-four ratio (TOF ratio below 0.75 and most subjects cannot sustain a head lift for a full 5 seconds). Measurement of tidal volume, minute volume and end tidal CO_2 are all essentially making the same assessment and they may return to normal values even though significant residual paralysis still exists particularly in unconscious patients, they indicate only that recovery is occurring. The response to airway obstruction, the ability to produce a negative inspiratory effort of at least -20 cm H_2O against an obstructed airway is a better indication that any residual block is not clinically significant.

6.   A C D

Caudal block is achieved by injecting local anaesthetic through the sacrococcygeal membrane into the extradural space in the sacral canal. The sacrococcygeal membrane covers the sacral hiatus, an opening caused by failure of the fusion of the 5th laminar arch. There is little likelihood of piercing the dura which normally ends at the lower border of S2. The average capacity of the sacral canal is 34 ml in males and 32 ml in females. It is a useful block for postoperative pain relief in children and the dose given is that generally recommended. The sympathetic outflow from the spinal cord ends at L2 whereas the sacral parasympathetic fibres leave with S2, 3&4.

7. **A B C**

Arthur E. Guedel (1883–1956) an American anaesthetist described his signs of anaesthesia in relation to the administration of open ether and spontaneous respiration, but they have a general application for all inhalational anaesthetics. Briefly they consist of:

First stage   Analgesia
Second stage   Excitement
Third stage   Surgical anaesthesia
  Plane 1   Onset of automatic respiration to cessation of eyeball movement
  Plane 2   Cessation of eyeball movement to start of intercostal paralysis
  Plane 3   Start to completion of intercostal paralysis
  Plane 4   Completion of intercostal paralysis to diaphragmatic paralysis
Fourth stage   Overdosage

The respiration is irregular in stage 2 and becomes regular and automatic at the start of stage 3. The pupils are usually dilated in the first stage due to emotion, in the second stage dilatation is the result of sympathetic stimulation of the dilator pupillae. In the third stage, plane 1, they return to normal and then progressively dilate again until the fourth stage. Premedication with opiates and atropine will affect these responses, miosis produced by the opiate usually predominates.

8. **B C E**

Nitrous oxide is produced by heating ammonium nitrate above 240°C in an iron retort. Ammonia, nitric acid, nitrogen, nitric oxide (NO) and nitrogen dioxide (NO_2) are also produced. The ammonia and nitric acid are reconstituted to ammonium nitrate and removed. The remaining gases pass through a series of scrubbers in which they are washed with water and caustic soda to remove all the NO and NO_2, this is carefully monitored but contamination of nitrous oxide has occurred and both contaminants are toxic. A crude test for contamination is to place a piece of moistened starch-iodide paper into a large syringe and draw in the suspect nitrous oxide along with 25% oxygen, if the gas is contaminated the paper turns blue within 10 minutes.

Full cylinders contain up to 80% of liquid nitrous oxide. In continuous use there is some fall in the gauge pressure, this results from the drop in temperature occurring as the liquid nitrous oxide evaporates and takes up latent heat, but if the cylinder is switched off and allowed to rewarm the pressure will rise once more to that of the full cylinder as long as liquid is still present. Only when all the liquid is exhausted will the gauge pressure fall steadily to zero.

9. **B C D**

Chronic hypo- or normo-chromic anaemia refractory to iron is a feature of rheumatoid arthritis, it may be further aggravated by GI bleeding from non-steroidal anti-inflammatory drugs used in treatment. The disease can affect the temporo-mandibular joints, the crico-arytenoids and the cervical spine, which may be fixed or subluxed and thus unstable especially when the patient is paralysed and anaesthetised. All or any of these conditions may make intubation difficult, in addition an unstable cervical spine puts the spinal cord at risk during intubation. Veins are thin and fragile particularly when steroids have been used, the shape of the hands may also contribute to difficulty with venepuncture. Coronary arteritis and postural hypotension are described but there is no reason why the patient should be in cardiac failure or hypotensive when lying flat.

10. **B D**

A haemoglobin result of under 10 g/dl is regarded as being an indication for cancelling a routine operation, although this might appear somewhat arbitrary, the presence of a more marked anaemia will cause the resting cardiac output to rise so that oxygen delivery to the tissues is maintained and the patient's CVS is therefore already under increased stress. Routine urine analysis is part of the standard preoperative preparation of patients and the presence of glucose or porphyrins which may cause the urine to turn brown or red on standing, requires further investigation. The values of potassium and bilirubin given are within the normal range.

11. **C E**

Opinions differ as to the period for which a tourniquet can be kept inflated, indicating perhaps that a cautious approach is appropriate. The following values err towards such caution.

	Arm	Leg
Inflation time	1 hour	2 hours
Inflation pressure	systolic BP+50 mmHg	twice systolic BP

Tourniquets are associated with an increased incidence of deep vein thrombosis and should not be used in patients with HbS, as acidosis and ischaemia in the limb may precipitate sickling. There is no contraindication to their use in spinal anaesthesia.

12. E

It may sometimes be necessary to maintain the patient in traction for 1-2 days whilst taking measures to improve their preoperative state, but it is not reasonable to keep an elderly patient bedbound for 7–10 days prior to operation. Postoperative mortality figures of more than 25% in the over eighties are quoted, bronchopneumonia being the commonest cause of death. Early mortality has been shown to be lower and postoperative arterial hypoxaemia minimal, following local anaesthesia with spinals or epidurals but there are practical difficulties in their use. Spinal block to T10 is adequate and unilateral block, produced by keeping the patient on his side for 10–15 minutes until the local has fixed, will reduce cardiovascular changes.

13. A B

Hiatus hernia and the presence of a nasogastric tube both compromise the integrity of the lower oesophageal sphincter and increase the risk of passive regurgitation. Metoclopramide speeds gastric emptying and when given preoperatively it can be useful in reducing the risk of aspiration.

14. A E

Non-depolarising or competitive muscle relaxants are characterised by fade and post-tetanic facilitation when tested with a nerve stimulator. The response of non-depolarising muscle relaxants to acidosis and alkalosis is not uniform but d-tubocurarine and pancuronium both have their action prolonged by acidosis and shortened by alkalosis, depolarising muscle relaxants are affected in the opposite way. Severe hypothermia (below 30°C) increases the block with non-depolarising muscle relaxants. Fasciculation and dual block are features of depolarising muscle blockade.

15. A D

In healthy individuals suxamethonium administration results in a rise in serum potassium of about 0.2-0.4 mmol/l and although pre-treatment with a small dose of d-tubocurarine may limit this rise, by itself d-tubocurarine has no effect on the serum potassium. Thiopentone produces a small decrease. In patients with extensive tissue breakdown such as trauma and burns (particularly between 3 and 10 weeks) the serum potassium is raised and suxamethonium may be particularly dangerous. In metabolic acidosis hydrogen ions enter cells in exchange for potassium ions thus raising plasma potassium. In alkalosis there is increased entry of potassium ions into cells as well as increased loss of potassium in the urine as hydrogen ions are retained, the plasma potassium therefore falls.

16. A B C D E
Fat embolism is often associated with fractures of the femur and tibia and its onset may be soon after the injury or delayed 2–3 days, it may be wrongly diagnosed as shock. The deposition of fat droplets in the lungs can lead to major respiratory problems, dyspnoea, pallor, cyanosis and pyrexia occur, the arterial PO_2 will fall and respiratory distress can develop. Fat may be found in the sputum and urine and the appearance of petechial haemorrhages over the upper chest, neck and in the conjunctiva is a characteristic sign, usually seen on the second or third day. Fat in the cerebral circulation and hypoxaemia can lead to mental deterioration and coma as well as being an additional cause of pyrexia.

17. A C E
Malignant hyperpyrexia is thought to result from a defect in the control mechanism for calcium release in the sarcoplasmic reticulum and mitochondria. Mannitol is a valuable osmotic diuretic and intravenous infusion of 10–20 g may be used in malignant hyperpyrexia to maintain renal output. Sodium bicarbonate is used to correct the acidosis that occurs with the greatly increased metabolism. Glucose and insulin may also be needed to treat hyperkalaemia resulting from cell breakdown. Dantolene, 1 mg/kg is the specific treatment.

18. C E
Nodal rhythm is commonly seen with inhalational anaesthesia and is seldom of serious significance, halothane causes a dose-dependent depression of the sinus node automaticity which will encourage the development of nodal or junctional rhythms. Fall in BP is not the cause but as with any arrhythmia, hypoxia may be the provoking factor and a careful check should be made to exclude it. Although sensory stimulation at light levels of halothane anaesthesia may lead to many types of arrhythmia, nodal rhythm is not one of them. The administration of atropine will usually abolish a nodal rhythm but it should be administered slowly and with care as it can produce more serious ventricular arrhythmias.

19. B D E

Halothane is not inflammable and may safely be used with soda lime in closed circuit anaesthesia. It causes dilatation in the cerebral circulation leading to a rise in ICP and when the ICP is already raised, as in head injuries, it should not be used. In the presence of halothane anaesthesia the threshold for dysrhythmias with catecholamines is lowered, if exogenous catecholamines are used as with adrenaline infiltration by the surgeon, this must be taken into account. Although opinions differ, a general recommendation is that not more than 10 ml of adrenaline solution at a maximum concentration of 1 in 100,000 should be used in a 10 minute period or 30 ml in 1 hour, the ventilation being normal. The reduction of uterine tone makes halothane an unsuitable agent at normal concentrations for caesarean section and ERCP.

20. A B E

The potential for venous air embolism exists whenever there is negative pressure in an open vein. Although usually considered in relation to head and neck surgery, it has been described in situations as diverse as varicose veins with steep head down tilt and breast surgery. Air passes through the venous circulation to the right side of the heart where its presence causes a loud 'mill-wheel' murmur; as it mixes with blood in the right ventricle, cardiac output and BP fall. When air passes into the pulmonary circulation gas exchange between the capillaries and alveolae is prevented by the presence of air in the blood and the end tidal CO_2 falls, obstruction to right sided outflow may also cause a rise in CVP. Nitrous oxide will tend to diffuse into the air in the circulation as it does into other air cavities in the body, this happens more rapidly than the air is absorbed and the effective gas embolus enlarges. Nitrous oxide should therefore be immediately discontinued and 100% oxygen administered whenever air embolism is suspected.

21. A C E

Atropine is an antimuscarinic drug, it is a competitive antagonist at the muscarinic receptor and does not affect the release of acetylcholine. It crosses the blood brain barrier, where it has an excitatory action and in toxic doses can cause convulsions. Conventional systemic doses have few ocular effects and it can be used as a premedicant in the presence of glaucoma.

22. E

Isoflurane produces less myocardial depression than halothane or enflurane and the fall in BP that occurs when it is used, results from a reduction in systemic vascular resistance. About 0.2% is metabolised in the liver (by comparison enflurane 2% and halothane 20% in round figures). It is not epileptogenic and the MAC of isoflurane in oxygen is 1.28% whereas that of halothane is 0.75%, therefore halothane is the more potent drug.

23. **C D E**
Heroin, or diamorphine, is synthetically produced by diacetylation of morphine, and methadone was first synthesised in Germany at the end of World War II. Raw opium contains more than 20 distinct alkaloids, the medicinally useful ones include: morphine, noscapine, codeine, papaverine and thebaine.

24. **A B C D E**
Chlorpromazine is a drug with many actions, and other phenothiazines with specific effects are usually more clinically useful. α-Adrenergic blockade is prominent and causes peripheral vasodilatation and a fall in BP. Some phenothiazines can produce extrapyramidal effects that include Parkinsonian muscle tremors, if not recognised as drug induced they may cause confusion in diagnosis. Chlorpromazine has a marked anti-emetic effect which is due to a competitive action on the chemoreceptor trigger zone, but large doses probably also act directly on the vomiting centre. It has a mild anticholinergic, atropine like action, as well as being a weak anti-histamine.

25. **A B E**
By definition this is the minimum alveolar concentration (MAC) of an anaesthetic agent required to produce lack of reflex response to skin incision in 50% of subjects. The MAC is unaffected by changes in the arterial PCO_2 or PO_2 over a wide range. It is affected by age; halothane has a MAC of 1.08% in infants and 0.64% at 81 years of age. Other inhalational anaesthetics reduce the MAC of any agent, the addition of 70% nitrous oxide reduces the MAC of halothane by about 60%. Narcotic analgesics lower MAC, in a non-additive fashion. Premedication with 10 mg of morphine lowers the MAC of halothane by about 7%. The blood/gas partition coefficient does not influence MAC, but there is a relationship between lipid solubility and MAC.

26. **A C D**
Halothane produces a fall in BP proportional to the depth of anaesthesia and this is mainly due to direct myocardial depression. There are a number of other actions on the CVS which also tend to lower the BP, there is a central depression of the vasomotor centre and sympathetic ganglion blockade is produced. But the total

peripheral resistance is unchanged at normocarbia, despite the obvious venous dilatation that is seen.

27. **A B C E**
Oxazepam is an active metabolite of diazepam as well as being available as a drug in its own right. Benzodiazepines in general are effective anticonvulsants and diazepam is of particular value in the management of status epilepticus. Chlormethiazole (Heminevrin) is a hypnotic with good anticonvulsant properties and has been employed for this purpose as an intravenous infusion, although it is more generally used for the symptoms of acute alcohol withdrawal. Thiopentone is also an anticonvulsant and has been used in status epilepticus, it is particularly recommended for convulsions occurring as a result of toxicity to local anaesthetics as it is likely to be immediately available in this situation.

28. **A D**
Verapamil and nifedipine are true calcium channel blocking drugs. Captopril is an angiotensin converting enzyme (ACE) inhibitor, propranolol is a β-blocking drug and hydralazine is an anti-hypertensive agent with a direct action on vascular smooth muscle.

29. **A C**
Contraindications are defined in two categories, relative and absolute, porphyria is an absolute contraindication to the use of barbiturates, including thiopentone. Constrictive pericarditis prevents the heart responding to the drop in systemic vascular resistance produced by thiopentone and a catastrophic fall in BP can result. Although the generation brought up on thiopentone may sometimes be heard to mumble that if given slowly and in a small enough dose thiopentone is always safe, in the context of a Part 1 MCQ it is contraindicated for constrictive pericarditis!

Many drugs have been accused of being triggering agents in malignant hyperpyrexia but thiopentone, opiates, diazepam, pancuronium and probably nitrous oxide are generally regarded as being safe. With MAOI drug therapy pethidine and related drugs are contraindicated, thiopentone can be used.

30. **A C**
Morphine stimulates histamine release and the secretion of catecholamines is increased due to stimulation of the adrenal medulla. Miosis occurs due to central stimulation of the pupillary fibres in the Edinger-Westphal nucleus and the impulse is carried in the oculomotor nerve, atropine can block the miosis. The sensitivity

of the respiratory centre to changes in the arterial PCO_2 is diminished by morphine, but at normal therapeutic dosage the arterial PCO_2 is not usually much raised. The high incidence of nausea and vomiting seen with morphine results from stimulation of the medullary chemoreceptor trigger zone and not from direct stimulation of the vomiting centre, although this does become more sensitive to vestibular activity produced by body movement.

31. A C

Propranolol blocks all β-receptors. Block of the $β_2$-receptors in the bronchioles may lead to bronchospasm and it is therefore contraindicated in asthmatics. In the heart the block of $β_1$-receptors reduces sympathetic drive and in paroxysmal nocturnal dyspnoea, a symptom of left sided cardiac failure, this may be dangerous. In atrial fibrillation, propranolol slows the ventricular rate but does not correct the dysrhythmia and although its use with digoxin requires care, there is no contraindication to the combination and in digoxin toxicity it may be specifically valuable when dysrhythmias are present. Changes in the serum potassium are relevant in digoxin administration but not with propranolol.

32. A

Cocaine is the exception amongst local anaesthetics in being a vasoconstrictor. Lignocaine and prilocaine have little effect on the vessels but the other local anaesthetics are vasodilators, hence the need to add vasoconstrictors such as adrenaline to them.

33. B

For accurate measurement of the BP it is essential that the width of the cuff should be in proportion to the size of the arm. The correct width is 20% greater than the diameter of the arm and the normal adult cuff is 13 cm wide. If the cuff is too narrow in relation to the arm excessive inflation pressure will have to be generated in the cuff in order to occlude the brachial artery, and this will give an erroneously high measurement of the BP. Slow deflation of the cuff and the position of the syphgmomanometer do not affect the reading. Severe atherosclerosis may alter the pulse wave form and raise systolic pressure, but it does not alter the accuracy of the measurement.

34. None correct

The saturated vapour pressure (SVP) depends only upon the nature of the liquid and the temperature, but the relationship to temperature is not linear, unlike a gas. At boiling point the SVP and atmospheric pressure are equal. But since the SVP is independent of barometric pressure, if the barometric pressure halves (e.g. at altitude) the concentration of a given vapour will double. The SVP of water at 37°C is 6.3 kPa (47 mmHg).

35.   B D
Poiseuille's equation states that with regard to laminar flow through tubes:

$$\text{Gas flow (Q)} = \frac{(P1\text{-}P2)\ r^4\ \pi}{8\ \eta\ l}$$

where (P1-P2) is the pressure drop across the tube, η the viscosity and l the length of the tube. Density is only a significant factor in turbulent flow.

36.   D
Nitrogen at high pressure has a narcotic effect and this is the reason for the use of helium for diving below about 70 m. Normal respiration is an example of laminar gas flow and viscosity is important in relation to laminar flow, but the viscosities of helium and nitrogen are similar. Helium is much less dense and in turbulent flow, as occurs in stridor and upper airway obstruction, this physical property is important; helium oxygen mixtures are therefore used in this clinical situation but this is not relevant to diving. The thermal conductivity of helium is six times greater than that of nitrogen, when helium is used in diving chambers the ambient temperature has to be kept around 30°C.

37.   C D
The oesophagus starts in continuity with the cricopharyngeus muscle at the level of C6, it passes into the thorax and lies in the posterior mediastinum – the space posterior to the pericardium and diaphragm. It is lined with stratified squamous epithelium and receives its motor supply from the vagus. Although anatomical measurements seem to ignore variation in overall size of the human population, the length of the oesophagus alone is stated to be 25 cm.

38.   B D
The anatomy of the first rib is of importance in relation to local blocks of the brachial plexus by the supraclavicular route and of the stellate ganglion. Moving along the upper surface of the rib from the front, the subclavian vein lies in a shallow groove anterior to the scalene tubercle into which scalenus anterior inserts. The sub-clavian artery crosses just behind the tubercle with the lower trunk of the brachial plexus immediately behind it, they form a deep groove. The scalenus medius then inserts posteriorly to these

structures into a roughened area on the postero-lateral area of the rib. The stellate ganglion is anterior to the head of the rib.

39. **A B D E**
The Valsalva manoeuvre is a forced expiration against a closed glottis or other obstruction and results in an increased intrathoracic pressure and a decreased venous return. Its importance to the anaesthetist is that the commencement of IPPV will lead to similar changes. The immediate response is a rise in systolic arterial pressure because the increase in intrathoracic pressure is added to the pressure of the blood in the aorta. The BP then falls as a result of a reduction in venous return, producing a drop in cardiac output. The fall in BP inhibits the baroreceptors, causing a tachycardia and a rise in peripheral resistance. When the Valsalva is released, the venous return and cardiac output are restored but the peripheral vessels are still constricted. The BP now rises above normal, the baroreceptors are stimulated and a bradycardia occurs until the BP returns to normal.

Normal Valsalva

40. **B C**
In the sympathetic nervous system the transmitter from pre-ganglionic to postganglionic fibres is acetylcholine, at the post-ganglionic nerve endings adrenaline and noradrenaline are released, except from the fibres going to the sweat glands where acetylcholine is released. In the gut, including the ileum, the smooth muscle is inhibited but the sphincters contract. Sympathetic stimulation causes pupillary dilatation, not miosis and the vagus only carries parasympathetic fibres. Guanethidine is an adrenergic neurone blocking agent, it depletes noradrenaline at the adrenergic nerve endings.

41. B C
Erythropoietin is a circulating glycoprotein made up of 166 amino acid residues. It is formed in response to hypoxia and reduced red cell volume, 85% is synthesised in the kidney, the remaining 15% coming from the liver. It promotes the conversion of certain erythropoietin sensitive stem cells to pro-erythroblasts.

42. A C D E
Carbon dioxide is transported in a variety of ways in the blood:
1. Dissolved in simple solution in both the plasma and red cells.
2. Most of the CO_2 is hydrolysed to carbonic acid in the red cells but this then dissociates to hydrogen ions and bicarbonate. Bicarbonate then diffuses into the plasma in exchange for chloride ions, the chloride shift.
3. As carbamino compounds in combination with haemoglobin and to lesser extent with plasma proteins.

43. A B C D E
Acute adaptation to the hypoxia of high altitude involves an increase in respiratory minute volume mediated by the peripheral chemoreceptors which are sensitive to hypoxia; the increased respiration leads to a reduction in the arterial CO_2 level. Initially this hyperventilation is reversible if oxygen is administered but after about a week it becomes irreversible. There is tachycardia and an increase in cardiac output but the CVS changes are much smaller than the respiratory. There is an increase in 2,3-DPG levels stimulated by hypoxia and this leads to a decreased affinity of haemoglobin for oxygen, making more oxygen available in the tissues and shifting the oxygen dissociation curve to the right, despite the fact that respiratory alkalosis would be tending to move the curve to the left. Polycythaemia develops over some months and increases the oxygen carrying capacity.

44. C E
The anterior pituitary secretes six hormones, adrenocorticotrophic hormone (ACTH), thyrotropin (TSH), growth hormone, follicle-stimulating hormone (FSH), luteinizing hormone (LH) and prolactin.

45. A B E
The oxygen dissociation curve is moved to the right by:

1. rise in hydrogen ions: acidosis, pH decrease;
2. rise in body temperature;
3. rise in PCO_2: in the pulmonary capillaries PCO_2 falls;

4.   rise in 2,3-DPG: in anaemia this is raised.

The arterial PO_2 falls with increasing age but this does not affect the dissociation curve.

46.   A B C
The 'a', 'c' and 'v' waves seen in the central venous pulse are produced by pressure changes in the right atrium which are transmitted to the great veins. The 'a' wave is caused by atrial systole which results in the regurgitation of some blood back into the great veins, it is absent in atrial fibrillation. The 'c' wave is caused by bulging of the tricuspid valve into the atrium during the phase of isometric ventricular contraction and the 'v' wave results from the pressure rise as blood flows into the RA but when the tricuspid valve opens and blood can enter the RV the pressure falls.

In inspiration, expansion of the chest creates a negative pressure which is transmitted to the veins in the chest and the central venous pressure falls. Clinically there is often a difference in the performance of the left and right sides of the heart. To obtain meaningful information when the problem is related to the left side, a balloon-tipped catheter can be used to measure the pulmonary capillary wedge pressure which is closely related to the left atrial pressure.

47. B E

The functional residual capacity (FRC) is the volume in the lungs at the end of expiration and represents the resting position of the lungs. There is probably a slight increase in FRC with age. Much more significant is the fall in FRC that occurs on moving from the upright to the supine position, and the further fall in FRC that occurs when a supine patient is anaesthetised. This fall on induction is of the order of 20% and is similar whether there is spontaneous breathing or IPPV. Closing capacity is the lung volume at which airways start to close. In contrast to FRC it does increase markedly with age, but is unchanged by position or anaesthesia. Because of the fall in FRC under anaesthesia, closing capacity may be greater than FRC with resultant atelectasis. This leads to shunting and decreased arterial PO_2 with an increased alveolar-arterial oxygen difference. (Closing capacity and closing volume are used somewhat loosely to mean the same thing. Strictly speaking closing capacity should be used and equals residual volume + closing volume.)

48. A B C D

Although sodium is reabsorbed along the whole length of the nephron, the greater part (about 70%) occurs in the proximal tubule. Glucose is completely reabsorbed as long as the plasma glucose remains within normal limits, its absorption is all from the proximal tubule. More than 90% of filtered potassium is reabsorbed in the proximal tubule and the urinary content of potassium is determined by the secretion of potassium into the collecting ducts and distal tubules under the control of aldosterone. In metabolic acidosis an increase in ammonia excretion occurs. Ammonia (NH_3) generated within the tubular cells passes into the lumen and in metabolic acidosis when there are surplus H^+ ions present, combines to form ammonium ions (NH^+_4). This 'holds' H^+ ions in the urine and promotes their excretion. ADH secretion responds to the changing osmolality of the plasma, it is secreted as a homeostatic mechanism well before true dehydration occurs.

49.   A B E

The respiratory centre in the medulla responds to changes in arterial PCO_2 and to a lesser extent pH. It does not respond to hypoxia which stimulates the peripheral chemoreceptors. In quiet breathing only the inspiratory muscles are in use, expiration then being a passive process. Vomiting is a complex reflex process including a number of actions, suspension of breathing and closure of the glottis are amongst these.

50.   C E

A hydrogen ion concentration of 100 nmol/l represents pH 7.0, at pH 7.4 it would be 40 nmol/l. The standard bicarbonate is the bicarbonate concentration in plasma at a PCO_2 of 5.3 kPa (40 mmHg) with the haemoglobin fully saturated and at a temperature of 37°C. Having thus corrected for respiratory factors it assesses the effect of metabolic factors on the plasma bicarbonate, normal values are 22–26 mmol/l. The base excess or deficit is the number of mmol/l required to titrate the pH back to 7.4, in making the correction clinically for a base deficit, it is regarded as being present in a proportion of the body fluids that represents one third of the body weight, (total body water=40% and ECF=20%), therefore:

$$\text{Bicarbonate required for correction in mmol} = \frac{\text{Base excess} \times \text{Body weight in kg}}{3}$$

The PaO_2 falls in old age and the $PaCO_2$ is reduced in hypothermia because of its increased solubility at low temperatures.

51.   E

In diabetes, hypoglycaemic coma induces the secretion of adrenaline in an attempt to release glycogen from the liver to raise the blood glucose, as a result there is a normal or raised BP and a full pulse. The skin and tongue are moist, this is in contrast with ketotic hyperglycaemia where osmotic diuresis leads to dryness and hypotension. The onset of ketoacidosis is slower, vomiting and abdominal pain often occur. Hypoglycaemia induces brisk reflexes and transient hemiparesis is a recognised complication particularly in the older patient, but bilateral extensor plantar responses are not seen. Cushing's syndrome with increased corticosteroids increases gluconeogenesis and raises blood glucose, this should make hypoglycaemic coma less probable.

52. B D
Increased skin pigmentation is a recognised feature of Addison's disease and may precede other features of the disease by many years, the mucous membranes of the mouth and conjunctivae may also become pigmented. Pregnancy leads to a rise in melanocyte stimulating hormone (MSH) which may result in a pigmentation of the midline of the abdomen (linea nigra), pigmentation of the nipples and patchy pigmentation of the face (the chloasma or 'mask' of pregnancy). Dark skinned, dark haired women are more likely to develop these patterns of pigmentation in pregnancy. In Cushing's syndrome the skin becomes thin and striae form, whereas in myxoedema or hypothyroidism it is thickened, coarse and sallow. Vitiligo is the presence of areas of patchy loss of pigment.

53. B
A bronchitic who chronically had an arterial PCO_2 of 8.0 kPa (60 mmHg) would have a compensatory metabolic alkalosis bringing the pH back towards normal, say to 7.35, with a base excess (BE) of say +6. In this case there has been no deterioration in the PO_2 or PCO_2 but his BE and standard bicarbonate (SBC) are normal. This must mean that there is an additional metabolic acidosis bringing his BE towards zero from what would be a 'normal' positive value for this patient. BE and SBC though very helpful in understanding acute changes can be difficult to interpret in chronic respiratory disease. Acute on chronic bronchitis would be characterised by a fall in pH with the BE and SBC staying the same. A metabolic acidosis is normally characterised by a negative BE and low SBC but in these peculiar circumstances where metabolic acidosis develops against a background of chronic (compensatory) metabolic alkalosis, the BE and SBC are normal.

54. B
Following transection of the spinal cord in man there is a period of about 3 weeks during which spinal shock occurs, all muscle tone is lost and there is flaccid paralysis. Muscle tone then returns but because all gamma efferent activity is lost, flexor tone exceeds extensor and the lower limbs flex. Shivering never occurs below the level of the lesion in spinal man. Micturition is a spinal reflex and is still present but the patient will have an automatic bladder. For a period following transection, variously stated to last from 36 hours to 36 weeks, suxamethonium administration may lead to dangerous rises in the serum potassium, but this is no longer a problem in long-standing paraplegia. Sweating is not lost, but can be markedly augmented as a result of uncontrolled sympathetic activity.

55. **A B C D E**
The four features of the condition are: pulmonary stenosis; VSD; dextroposition of the aorta which overides this defect; and right ventricular hypertrophy. Patients are deeply cyanosed and are subject to cyanotic and syncopal episodes particularly with exertion. There is a right to left shunt producing a systolic bruit and this in association with pulmonary stenosis leads to pulmonary oligaemia. Squatting after exercise is characteristic of the condition.

56. **A B E**
A raised serum amylase is characteristic of pancreatitis which is an important differential diagnosis, but there may also be a moderate rise with a perforation. Gastric and bowel stasis will increase the risk of inhalation of gastric contents and measures such as cricoid pressure would be essential at induction of anaesthesia. Increasing sepsis will raise the metabolic rate and oxygen delivery may be impaired due to atelectasis, the result will be increased lactic acid and a metabolic acidosis. The arterial PCO_2 is usually reduced or unchanged although opiate analgesia may mask this.

57. **C**
In sickle cell trait both normal adult haemoglobin, HbA, and between 25% and 45% of abnormal HbS are present in the blood, the condition is therefore designated HbAS. A Sickledex test screens for HbS and is positive in both homozygous and heterozygous individuals, only electrophoresis can differentiate between the two. Red cell survival is normal and anaemia is not usually present in uncomplicated HbAS, nor is splenomegaly. Unexplained haematuria is seen and there is also a reduced ability to concentrate urine. For patients with sickle cell trait a carefully conducted anaesthetic with continuous attention to adequate oxygen supply and continuous monitoring with a pulse oximeter are all that is required, measures such as exchange transfusion need only be considered for full sickle cell disease.

58. **A C**
Depression of the RST segment of the ECG is a characteristic change produced by digoxin even in normal dosage. Calcium gluconate is not of value in toxicity but if the serum potassium is low, the careful administration of potassium chloride either orally or intravenously may be beneficial but not if A-V block is present. Phenytoin and lignocaine are quite effective in suppressing ventricular arrhythmias, phenytoin is also effective for the treatment of atrial arrhythmias. Corticosteroids are of no value.

Although plasma levels of digoxin can be measured, they are not as reliable a guide to the severity of toxicity as other factors such as electrolyte imbalance, age, thyroid disease and renal function which will influence the severity of the toxicity.

59. A C

Donated blood is formally tested for hepatitis B, syphilis and HIV antibody. Malaria parasites can survive in stored blood to be transmitted to a recipient, this risk is minimised by questioning donors and excluding those that have had malaria or who have recently travelled in endemic areas.

60. B D

In hyperkalaemia the P wave amplitude is reduced and the P waves may be absent. The PR interval may be increased leading to atrial standstill. The T waves become large and 'tented' and QRS duration is increased. Associated low serum sodium will accentuate these changes. Prominent U waves are seen in hypokalaemia.

THE WRITTEN PAPERS : OUTLINE ANSWERS

WRITTEN PAPER 1

1. Describe the anatomical structures encountered in the passage of a needle for spinal anaesthesia.

A straightforward short anatomical question but details, particularly of the deeper layers must be thorough.

OUTLINE

In the adult the spinal cord ends at L2 and spinal puncture must be below this level. From the surface, in the midline at levels between L2 and S1.

Skin and subcutaneous tissue.

Supraspinous ligament, thick and tough, joining the tips of the spinous processes of the vertebrae.

Interspinous ligament, thin layer between the spines.

Ligamentum flavum, yellow elastic tissue, thick and tough particularly in the lumbar region, running from lamina above to that below.

Extradural space, contains loose fat and plexus of veins, normally at negative pressure and really a potential space.

Dura mater, strong fibrous layer with fibres running longitudinally.

Subdural space, potential space between the dura and arachnoid maters, contains capillaries and lymphatics.

Arachnoid mater, thin transparent sheath closely applied to dura.

Subarachnoid space, contains CSF, nerves of the cauda equina and filum terminale (the continuation of the pial covering of the cord extending down through dura to the coccyx).

If the needle passes on, it goes through the dural layers anteriorly and pierces the posterior longitudinal ligament before hitting the vertebral body.

2. Describe the physiological effects of passive hyperventilation.

The question requires one to define the term passive hyperventilation and then describe the effects on various physiological systems.

OUTLINE

Definition: Ventilation of a patient to a lower arterial PCO_2 (normal 5.3 kPa). Passive implies the subject is not breathing spontaneously.

Effects:

1. Blood gases, PCO_2 decreased, pH raised, standard bicarbonate unchanged at first, PO_2 increased because of the lower PCO_2 (see ideal gas equation).
2. Renal compensation, increased excretion of bicarbonate bringing pH back towards normal (not reaching normal), standard bicarbonate falls.
3. Electrolytes, plasma potassium tends to fall as pH rises (potassium moves into cells to replace hydrogen ions), ionised calcium decreases (but total calcium rises slightly).
4. Respiratory centre, decrease or abolition of respiratory drive via central chemoreceptors.
5. Haemoglobin oxygen dissociation curve, shifted to left, decreasing O_2 available at tissues.
6. Neurones, increased excitability due to low ionised calcium: carpopedal spasm.
7. Cardiovascular, cardiac output decreases, vasoconstriction, uterine blood flow may fall, cerebral blood flow decreased with hypocapnia, ICP decreased, consciousness may be lost.

3. **A patient with chronic bronchitis is to have a general anaesthetic, what tests of respiratory function would be of value and what would be the significance of the results obtained?**

There are 2 parts to this question:

a) what tests
b) significance of the results

These are probably best dealt with together with a paragraph for each test.

OUTLINE

Introduction: Purpose of tests not diagnostic, but to assess severity, reversibility and progress of disease. Helps to decide on timing of anaesthesia, type of anaesthetic and seniority of anaesthetist. The simplest tests can be done at the bedside and can be repeated to assess preoperative treatment and postoperative progress.

Peak expiratory flow rate (PEFR) a simple bedside test, normal adult value 400 to 700 l/min.

Forced expiration (Vitalograph), FEV_1 and FVC but values obtained must be related to patient size and sex. FEV_1/FVC ratio normal value 70%, reduced in obstructive disease but in restrictive disease ratio unchanged or slightly increased because both values are reduced. Can be repeated after salbutamol to look for reversibility. If these are within normal limits one need not proceed to more complex tests.

Arterial blood gases, chronic bronchitics have a chronic respiratory acidosis, metabolic alkalosis and hypoxaemia. Estimation of pre-operative values will show if the patient is in best condition and will guide postoperative O_2 therapy and in severe cases the need for postoperative ventilation. Knowing the patient's 'normal' PCO_2 is important in reversal at the end of the operation.

Lung volumes, FRC, TLC and RV are all increased in emphysema which can co-exist with chronic bronchitis. If there is a large difference between FRC by helium dilution and thoracic gas volume by body plethysmography, this suggests areas of unventilated lung e.g. bullae, gas trapping.

Other specialised tests, carbon monoxide transfer factor and flow volume loops.

4. **What are the actions of intravenous barbiturates on the cardiovascular system? Discuss briefly their clinical significance.**

A fairly straightforward question in 2 parts. The word "briefly" in the second part indicates that more weight should be given to the first part.

OUTLINE

Thiopentone and methohexitone do not differ significantly in their cardiovascular effects, therefore consider them together.

CVS effects - vary with dose, speed of injection, bolus or infusion, age of patient and physical fitness.

Myocardial contractility	modest decrease
Systemic vascular resistance	little change
Venous capacitance	increased, blood pooling
Cardiac output	modest decrease
Blood pressure	modest decrease

Heart rate	increase
Rhythm	no change

Local effects of intra-arterial injection of thiopentone - spasm, necrosis.

Anaphylactic or anaphylactoid reaction - rare, severe CVS collapse, usually previous sensitisation.

Clinical significance - normally effects are transient and are limited by the increase in heart rate but they can be much worse in those who cannot compensate, hypovolaemia, cardiac or adreno-cortical insufficiency, constrictive pericarditis, tight valvular stenosis, heart block. Administer cautiously. Effective in one arm-brain circulation time, therefore dose can be titrated to assess effect. Enquire for pain with thiopentone in case of intra-arterial injection.

5. **What are the indications for awake intubation in the adult? Describe the local anaesthetic technique that you would use for this procedure.**

Awake intubation is less often practiced in the UK than in the USA and indications will therefore vary according to local opinion, they can be listed briefly with the most relevant first. There are a number of alternatives for the local anaesthetic technique, for instance lignocaine spray can be used throughout but in an examination answer one should not make it too simple, the procedure below can be recommended.

OUTLINE

Indications (these are relative rather than absolute): the technique requires patient co-operation and full explanation
1. anatomically deformed upper airway particularly if sedation or anaesthesia may lead to loss of airway
2. immobile neck e.g. ankylosing spondylitis
3. inability to open mouth
4. respiratory failure requiring IPPV (to minimise use of drugs)
5. to avoid aspiration with a full stomach (as an alternative to cricoid pressure).

Local anaesthetic technique:

Upper airway, via nose 4-10% cocaine spray to both nostrils + 2% lignocaine spray to back of throat, or via mouth 60 mg amethocaine lozenge to suck, given 30 minutes beforehand.
Larynx above cords, superior laryngeal nerve which supplies the larynx above the cords can be blocked by the application of 8-10% cocaine to

each pyriform fossa on a dental swab held in Krause's forceps.
Larynx below the cords, (recurrent laryngeal nerve) crico-thyroid or trans-tracheal injection of 2-3 ml of 4% lignocaine during inspiration.

Absorption of local anaesthetic drugs from mucosal surfaces is rapid and maximum dosage levels must not be exceeded. If local anaesthesia is used with a full stomach the laryngeal reflexes should not be totally abolished.

6. **Describe your anaesthetic management of a 25 year old woman, who is 35 weeks pregnant and has developed appendicitis.**

An amalgamation of a standard emergency anaesthetic with the addition of the problems of late pregnancy.

OUTLINE

Preoperative visit, routine checks with particular reference to history of any problems during pregnancy, present condition particularly vomiting, past personal and family anaesthetic history, drugs, allergies; examine for dehydration and general fitness, check foetal heart; FBC and U&E's. Explain procedures, reassure, prescribe premedication as necessary. Give 30 ml of 0.3 Molar sodium citrate shortly before anaesthesia.

Induction, place patient on operating table with lateral tilt to prevent vena caval compression; set up IV infusion; check intubation equipment and suction, fully pre-oxygenate; induce anaesthesia with thiopentone apply cricoid pressure and then give suxamethonium; intubate, check tube placement.

Operation, maintain anaesthesia with usual anaesthetic drugs and relaxants (volatile agents which relax the uterus may be beneficial). Avoid maternal hyperventilation which may reduce placental blood flow; monitor ECG and BP and consider continuous monitoring of foetal heart.

Post-operation, ensure full reversal of relaxants, extubate in left lateral head down and keep on side until fully awake; give oxygen for at least 4 hours.

Local anaesthesia, for instance epidural anaesthesia could be used.

7. **Discuss the causes and treatment of a sudden rise in blood pressure during general anaesthesia for a laparotomy.**

This is very much a practical question and it is important to show in your answer that you would look for common causes first and leave rarities to the end. Treatment depends very much on the cause so they should be dealt with together.

OUTLINE

1. Light anaesthesia, check nitrous oxide supply and vaporiser not empty, deepen anaesthesia with volatile agent or opiate.
2. Pre-existing hypertension, either undiagnosed or treatment stopped pre-operatively. Laryngoscopy is often the stimulus. IV β-blockers may be needed.
3. Hypercarbia (Capnograph), check breathing circuit and patient airway, CO_2 flowmeter not fully closed, with circle soda lime not exhausted, gas flows and ventilation adequate.
4. Hypoxia (Oximeter), importance of checking machine, checks as above, assess colour of fresh bleeding in wound and if necessary allow patient to breathe air.
5. Drugs, ketamine, cyclopropane, pancuronium, IV injection of vasopressor by surgeon.
6. Preoperative drugs, monoamine oxidase inhibitors interacting with opiates, clonidine rebound.
7. Fluid overload, stop infusion.
8. Hypoglycaemia, give dextrose.
9. Hormone secreting tumour, toxic goitre, phaeochromocytoma, carcinoid. Nitroprusside probably required.

WRITTEN PAPER 2

1. Describe the anatomical structures below the epiglottis seen during bronchoscopy.

The anatomy of the airway is asked about in a variety of ways, its anatomy and nerve supply should be known thoroughly.

OUTLINE

1. Laryngeal opening, lateral to the epiglottis on each side are the aryepiglottic folds containing the cuneiform and corniculate cartilages and posteriorly the arytenoid cartilages.
2. Enter the vestibule of the larynx which reaches down to the vestibular folds or false cords, pass through the gap between, the rima vestibuli.
3. Enter the saccule of the larynx with the vocal cords below, thyroid

cartilage in front and at the side, and the vocal process of the arytenoids behind, pass through the gap between the cords, the glottis (narrowest part of the airway in adults, in children the subglottic region is narrower).

4. Continue through the cricoid ring into the trachea with C-shaped cartilages lying anteriorly and laterally, after 10-12 cm in adults reach the carina.

5. Right side - main bronchus branches at 25° (distances from carina) 2.5 cm at 3 o'clock - upper lobe bronchus divides into 1. apical 2. anterior 3. posterior 4.0 cm at 12 o'clock - middle lobe bronchus divides into 4. medial 5. lateral 4.5 cm at 6 o'clock - lower lobe bronchus divides into 6. apical 7. medal (cardiac) 8. anterior 9. lateral 10. posterior.

6. Left side, main bronchus branches at 45°
    5.5 cm at 9 o'clock - upper lobe bronchus divides into 1. apical 2. anterior 3. posterior + lingula 4. superior 5. inferior
    5.0 cm at 3 o'clock - lower lobe bronchus divides into 6. apical 7. anterior 8. lateral 9. posterior (no medial on left).

2. **Describe the physiological mechanisms by which arterial hypoxaemia may occur.**

The logical way to tackle this question is by following the transfer of oxygen from the atmosphere to the mitochondria and noting how it may be diminished at each stage. This question only asks for arterial hypoxaemia so tissue hypoxaemia need not be considered.

OUTLINE

1. Breathing hypoxic mixture, high altitudes or unusual gas mixture.
2. Hypoventilation due to:
      respiratory centre depression
      spinal cord lesions
      anterior horn cells (polio)
      neuropathy (Guillain-Barre)
      neuromuscular (myasthenia)
      chest wall (crushed or flail chest)
      upper airway obstruction
3. Diffusion impairment e.g. interstitial fibrosis acting as a barrier to diffusion.
4. Shunt, blood reaching the arterial system without passing through ventilated lung, shunt may be:
      extrapulmonary (right to left shunts in the heart)
      intrapulmonary (consolidated pneumonic lobule)

shunts are the only cause of arterial hypoxaemia not improved by 100% oxygen.
5. Ventilation perfusion inequality, this is the main cause in many lung disorders (chronic bronchitis, pulmonary embolism).
6. Reduction of oxygen content in the blood (but not necessarily PaO_2 by anaemia, methaemoglobinaemia, carbon monoxide poisoning).

3. Describe briefly the physical principles involved in the functioning of calibrated anaesthetic vaporisers.

A short question but be sure to stick to the physical principles.

OUTLINE

1. Splitting ratio, the gas flow must be split precisely so that a set proportion passes through the vaporising chamber and the rest by-passes it.
2. Saturated vapour, gas passing through the vaporising chamber must be fully saturated with the anaesthetic agent, the chamber therefore contains wicks and baffles to ensure that the gas is fully saturated. The quantity of anaesthetic present will then be the saturated vapour pressure which depends only on temperature, at room temperature of 20°C this is known.
3. Latent heat of vaporisation, vaporisation requires heat and the remaining liquid will cool, this must be compensated for as the SVP falls with temperature and less anaesthetic agent is vaporised.

Methods:
   a. 'heat sink', vaporiser constructed of good heat conducting metal and having a large surface area.
   b. temperature compensation devices e.g. bimetallic valves.

4. Compare and contrast the pharmacological effects of vecuronium and d-tubocurarine.

The best way to compare and contrast is to take each aspect and discuss the effects of both drugs pointing out similarities and differences. You are only asked about pharmacological effects so history, manufacture, excretion etc. are not required.

OUTLINE

Both are non-depolarising neuromuscular blockers and show the characteristic pattern of fade and post-tetanic facilitation on peripheral nerve stimulation.

Potency, vecuronium 0.1 mg/kg approximately 5-6 times as potent as d-tubocurarine.

Onset, vecuronium faster than d-tubocurarine, intubating conditions in 1 to 2 minutes but over 3 minutes with d-tubocurarine, increasing the dose does not speed onset.

Duration, dose dependent but with equipotent doses vecuronium lasts 20-30 minutes and d-tubocurarine 30-40 minutes.

Potentiation, volatile anaesthetic agents especially enflurane, potentiate d-tubocurarine more than vecuronium.

Cumulation, with repeated doses, time and speed of recovery are not increased with vecuronium but they are with d-tubocurarine.

Recovery, once recovery beings, time from 25% to 75% of control twitch height is 11-12 minutes with vecuronium, longer with d-tubocurarine.

Reversal, both reversed by anticholinergics.

CVS effects, vecuronium devoid of CVS effects, d-tubocurarine decreases the BP by ganglion blockade.

Histamine release, none with vecuronium but occurs with d-tubocurarine and may cause bronchospasm in asthmatics.

Central effects, neither drug crosses the blood-brain or placental barriers.

5. **Describe in detail the management of intravenous regional anaesthesia (Bier's block) in the upper limb.**

Preparation is as important as the technique.

OUTLINE

Preparation of patient, see the patient and check for contraindications — allergy to local anaesthetic drugs, sickle disease, Raynauds, scleroderma, severe neurological disease and possibly local infection. Explain the procedure to the patient, arrange for him to be starved and premedicate if necessary. Check equipment, full resuscitation equipment *immediately* to hand including method to administer oxygen by IPPV and to perform intubation, IV infusion equipment, drugs for convulsions, suction. Check the BP, have an open vein in other limb.

Technique

1. apply double cuff to arm
2. insert butterfly or cannula into distal vein (back of hand) and secure very firmly
3. exsanguinate the limb, if not painful Esmarch bandage or pneumatic exsanguinator, otherwise elevation for 3-5 minutes with occlusion of the brachial artery
4. inflate the upper cuff to 100 mmHg above systolic BP, note the time
5. inject prilocaine 0.5% plain solution, 3 mg/kg slowly
6. check the adequacy of the block

If necessary after 5 minutes the lower cuff may be inflated and then the upper cuff deflated. Cuff deflation, wait at least 20 minutes and if in doubt or patient is frail let down and re-inflate a number of times.

6. A woman in shock is thought to have an ectopic pregnancy, describe briefly your anaesthetic management.

Precisely the sort of situation that a Registrar at a DGH would be expected to deal with, as the exam is supposed to assess the candidate's ability for such a post, the written answer should be clear and to the point.

OUTLINE

Resuscitation must precede anaesthesia but this should be done quickly as only surgery can stop the bleeding. If BP low give oxygen. Initial assessment of blood loss, obtain good venous access, if shock is severe set up CVP and do blood gas to check for acidosis. Give IV fluid mainly colloid but also some crystalloid, FBC and cross-match 6 units and give blood when this is available. Look for filling of jugular veins, warming-up of periphery with filling of veins and pink colour, or CVP to satisfactory positive level. BP of over 100 mmHg if possible.

Premedication, should be minimal, atropine only; oxygen during transport to theatre.

Induction: ECG and BP recorder, induce on operating table if concerned: pre-oxygenation, cricoid pressure, whatever induction agent is chosen it must be administered cautiously, ketamine may be indicated in very shocked. Suxamethonium for intubation, theoretically relaxation of the abdominal muscles releases tamponade effect and causes more bleeding; surgeon should be scrubbed up and ready.

Maintenance: avoid all cardiac depressant drugs e.g. volatile anaesthetic agents at least until surgical control of haemorrhage, blood replacement intra-operatively (haematocrit 30%), fresh frozen plasma and calcium if tranfusion over 4 units.

Post-operation: extubate on side, head down, assess urine output and encourage if necessary, check haematocrit and continue oxygen.

7. **How may hypercarbia develop during anaesthesia, what clinical changes may result?**

There are a number of ways of approaching this question, one would be:

1. During spontaneous respiration
2. During IPPV
3. Others

Spend time to think of as many causes as possible. For clinical changes that result, go through the systems of the body, although most will be in the respiratory and cardiovascular systems.

OUTLINE

During spontaneous respiration:

Drugs depressing respiration, opiates in premedication or anaesthesia, barbiturates.

Deep anaesthesia, halothane for instance is a respiratory depressant and deep levels of anaesthesia lead to marked hypercarbia. Respiratory function, myasthenia, scoliosis.

Mechanical causes, airway obstruction, head down tilt especially in the obese, poor positioning e.g. prone, surgical retractors, assistants leaning on the chest.

Rebreathing, insufficient fresh gas flow for the circuit, increased dead space e.g. large mask on a small child, soda lime exhausted.

During IPPV:
Inadequate settings, ventilator set to insufficient minute volume for the patient, particularly likely with large patients or those with fever.

Leaks, in the ventilator or circuit. Dead space too large.

Others:
CO_2 administration, CO_2 flowmeter inadvertently switched on, CO_2 absorption when this gas is used for laparoscopy

Patient causes, increased CO_2 production e.g. fever, fitting.

Clinical changes:
CVS, increased catecholamine release, raises cardiac output, BP up, tachycardia, pulse full and bounding, local vasodilatation increasing bleeding, increased chance of arrhythmias especially with halothane.

RS, when possible increased respiratory drive leading to increased minute volume, respiratory acidosis moving the oxygen dissociation curve to the right.

CNS, cerebral blood flow increased leading to an increase in intra-cranial pressure, high concentrations of CO_2 have an anaesthetic action.

WRITTEN PAPER 3

1. **Describe the relations of the internal jugular vein, what are the common complications of internal jugular cannulation.**

In anatomical questions, a diagram well labelled can save many words. Unless you are completely unable to draw this is recommended. The key word in the second half is common: at least 23 different complications have been described, you are not expected to list them all!

OUTLINE

Internal jugular vein is the continuation of the sigmoid sinus, runs from base of skull to join the subclavian behind sternal end of the clavicle forming brachiocephalic vein.

Relations:

Posteriorly: sympathetic chain, prevertebral fascia, muscles and trans-verse processes. At root of neck subclavian artery is deep to vein, as are phrenic, vagus nerves and dome of pleura. Thoracic duct on left.

Medial: lies in the carotid sheath with internal carotid artery antero-medial high up (IX, X, XI and XII between) and the common carotid and vagus medial lower down. Superficial: high up deep to parotid, lower down under cover of sternomastoid.

Complications:

Specific to this technique and related to the anatomy:
    carotid artery puncture (the commonest)
    pneumothorax (less risk with high approach and short needle)
    vertebral artery puncture
    nerve damage: Horner's (sympathetic plexus), phrenic, vagus
    thoracic duct (on left)

General complications:
    air embolism (importance of head down)
    haematoma
    sepsis
    thrombosis, thrombophlebitis

2. **Compare the physiological response to the infusion of 1 litre of normal saline with that resulting from the infusion of 1 litre of plasma.**

The sort of question that produces a chaotic answer if not carefully planned. The initial response is similar with both but the later effects are different.

OUTLINE

Both solutions enter the intravascular compartment which has a fluid volume of 3.5 l (plasma), normal saline contains 151 mmol of sodium and chloride and will slightly raise their plasma concentrations, the colloid content of plasma keeps it in this compartment, whereas normal saline will tend to pass out into the interstitial fluid which has a volume of 10.5 l and be held here by its sodium content.

Initial response: heart - increasing intravascular volume, CVP rises, stroke volume rises, cardiac output rises (risk of overload with rapid infusion leading to pulmonary oedema particularly with plasma).

Plasma osmolarity not altered therefore osmoreceptors not stimulated but increased volume stimulates low pressure receptors in atria, large veins and pulmonary vessels; ADH secretion reduced, more so with plasma.

Later response: renal, increased renal blood flow and increased mean renal BP depress the renin, angiotensin mechanism and aldosterone secretion falls. GFR increased and with reduced aldosterone and ADH, urinary excretion of salt and water increased. With plasma infusion, the oncotic pressure will rise as water passes into the tubules and reabsorption of fluid is thereby increased.

Capillaries - with normal saline plasma osmotic pressure falls and reabsorption of fluid in the venous end of the capillary is reduced so that there is a net loss of fluid into the interstitial fluid; with plasma infusion the oncotic pressure is maintained and this does not happen.

Result: normal saline diffused into larger volume of interstitial fluid and also increased urinary output so that its effects are short lived; but plasma has remained in intravascular compartment and represents a very marked increase in its volume, therefore CVS changes maintained while level of plasma proteins is readjusted through decreased production.

3. **Describe the Mapleson classification for anaesthetic circuits indicating to which group the circuits in common use belong.**

A very straightforward question and one which you could probably answer in less than the allotted time by the use of diagrams. Once you have answered, use the time saved on another question. Further discussion of Mapleson circuits (e.g. of gas flows which was not asked) will not score extra marks in a close marking system. Remember to label the diagrams.

OUTLINE

Draw the systems which are in all the textbooks.

A. Magill attachment, Lack system is a coaxial version with expired gas flowing up the central tube.

B. & C. Only used in resuscitation or transport of patients.

D. The manual mode of many ventilators, Bain circuit is the coaxial version with fresh gas flowing up the centre.

E. Ayre's T piece for paediatrics, no bag.

F. Jackson Rees version of E with open bag at the end.

4. What is the safe maximum dose of the commonly used local anaesthetic drugs? What may occur clinically with overdosage.

A short table will cover the first part but remember to give doses with and without adrenaline. The second part should be detailed but note you are not asked for the treatment.

OUTLINE

	plain	with adrenaline
Lignocaine	3 mg/kg	7 mg/kg
Bupivacaine	2 mg/kg	—
Prilocaine	5 mg/kg	8 mg/kg
Cinchocaine	1-2 mg/kg	
Cocaine (topical)	1.5 mg/kg	

Higher concentrations more toxic than weaker ones. Route of administration effects uptake and toxicity.

Overdosage

General signs: pallor particularly around mouth, nausea, sweating, yawning and drowsiness often precede true overdosage.

CNS: stimulation followed by depression; anxiousness, restlessness, hysterical behaviour, vertigo, tremor leading on in severe cases to convulsions and respiratory depression.

CVS: hypotension, badycardia with feeble pulse leading to cardiac failure and arrest (with cocaine VF may occur without warning).

RS: apnoea in severe cases due to central depression and respiratory muscle paralysis.

5. Discuss the advantages and disadvantages of spinal and general anaesthesia for a patient requiring surgery for a fractured neck of femur.

This is quite a topical question because of recent claims that spinal anaesthesia decreases mortality in patients with fractured hips. A good discussion is more than merely a list of pros and cons, it involves debate and argument. The outline below lists the points which should be covered.

OUTLINE

Make the general point: these patients are usually elderly and infirm.

Spinal: advantages, little effect on respiration, good for bad chest, decreased postoperative hypoxaemia, less risk of aspiration, some postoperative analgesia, reduced blood loss, decreased incidence of thrombo-embolism, minimises period without food and water, less problems with diabetics, some series show decreased early mortality but no difference at one year. Disadvantages, takes a little longer than GA, difficulty of positioning a patient in pain both for block and on operating table, there is a failure rate, risk of fall in BP and need for vasopressors, nausea, vaso-vagal attack may occur in awake patient, patient may dislike being awake, frequent coughing in severe bronchitic, postoperative headache (use fine needle).

GA: advantages, quicker, no failure rate, hypotension (may be avoided by choice of technique). Disadvantages, greater incidence of postoperative chest complications and hypoxaemia, risks of full stomach in emergency case, more thrombo-emboli.

6. **Discuss the problems posed for the anaesthetist by patients with narcotic addiction.**

A complete answer is the result of bringing together many small points but stick to specific anaesthetic problems.

OUTLINE

Personality: often deceitful, difficult and aggressive, premedication may need to be heavy and include sedative agents

Venous access: nearly always a problem due to repeated thrombophlebitis and loss of veins, look at feet and legs or external jugular; if inhalational induction required second stage may be difficult.

Infection risk: abscesses, hepatitis, AIDs (wear gloves and take particular care to avoid pricking oneself).

Patient's general state: nutritional state often poor leading to risk of infection postoperatively, right sided infective endocarditis may occur, pulmonary disease due to septic pulmonary emboli leading to asthma and pulmonary oedema, unexpected hypotension may occur during anaesthesia. Withdrawal: cramps, vomiting and diarrhoea due to withdrawal may confuse clinical picture, difficult to know whether to treat symptoms or give narcotic.

Post-operation: analgesic requirements difficult to assess, tolerance to narcotics, patients may exaggerate pain or interfere with wound to get more narcotic.

7. What action would you take when you find yourself unexpectedly, unable to intubate a patient at emergency Caesarean section.

Every trainee should know a failed intubation drill in advance, this should therefore be easy to answer. Note the question says ' What action would you take': do not waste time discussing different strategies, choose one and give it. The other key words in the question are 'unexpectedly' and 'emergency'. A discourse on anticipating difficulty is not required. Emergency implies that waking the patient up and giving a regional block will be too slow, though this possibility should be mentioned. Tunstall's plan is the best known.

OUTLINE

Make the decision to abandon repeat attempts at intubation promptly.

1. Maintain cricoid pressure.
2. Place head down in left lateral position, get help from those around
3. Oxygenate by IPPV via face mask and oral airway, aspirate pharynx
4. If still obstructed try releasing cricoid pressure
5. If ventilation is easy establish anaesthesia with nitrous oxide, oxygen and ether by spontaneous ventilation. If you are unfamiliar with ether, halothane or enflurane can be used, local anaesthetic infiltration by the surgeon may also be given.
6. Pass stomach tube via mouth, aspirate, instill 20 ml 0.3 molar sodium citrate.
7. Level table, place patient supine with left lateral tilt and wedge, proceed with operation under spontaneous ventilation.

Additional points: if the patient is too light abandon attempts to pass the gastric tube, syntocinon can be infused if there is undue bleeding, pethidine can be given and halothane reduced after delivery, if unable to ventilate effectively allow mother to wake up, maternal mortality is more disastrous than perinatal mortality.

Reference: Tunstall, Anaesthesia 1976, vol. 31, p.850

ANSWERS TO THE CLINICAL CASE HISTORIES

Case History 1

Commentary

1. He is hypertensive, but a single reading should not be relied upon and he should be on a 4 hourly chart to see if his pressure settles.

2. The chest X-ray shows cardiac enlargement and unfolding of the aorta. The ECG shows left ventricular hypertrophy as evidenced by:
   a) tall R waves in V_4 (32 mm) and V_5 (22 mm).
   b) deep S waves in V_1 (14 mm), these can be confused with Q waves.
   c) S in V_1 and R in V_5 = 36 (greater than 35 mm)
      and left ventricular strain as evident by T wave inversion and ST depression in V_{4-6}.

3. The patient has serious hypertension which should be brought under control before he is anaesthetised, particularly for an elective procedure such as wisdom teeth. This operation should be postponed. There is now plenty of evidence that untreated hypertensives have higher anaesthetic morbidity than their treated counterparts.

4. This technique is not appropriate for a patient with cardiovascular disease. Cocaine, raised CO_2 and halothane all make ventricular ectopics more likely.

5. The fresh gas flow recommended by Bain for spontaneous breathing with a Bain circuit is 100 ml/kg and others have recommended higher flows than this. 6 l/min for an 80 kg man is certainly too low and is likely to result in hypercarbia.

6. Bigeminy: alternate beats are ventricular ectopics.

7. In addition to factors listed in 4 the surgical stimulus of dental extraction itself may cause arrhythmias. Halothane and raised CO_2 sensitise the myocardium to the effects of endogenous adrenaline which may be released if anaesthesia is light. The CO_2 may be raised because of the inadequate fresh gas flow with the Bain circuit. Partial obstruction will lead to a rising CO_2 and can occur during dental manipulation, movement of the head and the pack. Hypertension results if CO_2 is retained and may be particularly dangerous in this patient. Myocardial oxygen demand is increased while at the same time the increased ventricular wall tension may result in sub-

endocardial ischaemia if there is coronary atheroma. All of which emphasise the fact that this patient should not have been anaesthetised until his hypertension was controlled.

Case History 2

Commentary

1. She has hyperosmolar diabetic coma, characterised by the high blood glucose and glycosuria with no ketones in the urine. The urea and electrolyte concentrations are raised because she is dehydrated. Serum albumin is raised for the same reason as are the haemoglobin and haematocrit (but see below). The leucocytosis suggests infection. The blood gases show a mild metabolic acidosis which would be consistent with her ill and dehydrated state. The acidosis would be much more severe if due to diabetic ketosis.

2. a) Osmolality = $(2 \times Na + 2 \times K + glucose + urea) = 374$ mmol/l (normal 290). The high osmolality draws water out of cells which is why the change in haematocrit is not a good guide to the amount of dehydration in these circumstances.

   b) Dehydration can be estimated by comparing the raised serum albumin (57 g/l) with an estimate of the albumin before illness, say 40 g/l. Then the fall in ECF volume = $(1 - 40/57) = 30\%$. Her ECF volume would normally be about 15 l, so the deficit in ECF is 4.5 l and there is a further deficit in intracellular volume which is harder to estimate.

3. It is essential to correct the dehydration and metabolic chaos before embarking on anaesthesia and surgery. Diabetic gangrene is not an immediate life threatening emergency and the amputation can wait 24 hours which will be needed to correct the abnormalities.

4. 0.45% saline must be given to correct the dehydration and hypernatraemia. This must be done cautiously as too rapid a shift of water back into brain cells may exacerbate the cerebral state. Continuous insulin infusion will bring down the blood sugar and as this happens potassium will move into cells and potassium will have to be added to the infusion. Frequent electrolyte and glucose estimations are essential. (BMstix would be satisfactory.) CVP measurement will aid volume replacement. Broad spectrum antibiotics should be given to cover the infection. Once blood glucose is approaching normal the

operative period can be covered by an infusion of 10% dextrose 500 ml 4 hourly with soluble insulin 10 units and 10 mmol KCl. The insulin can be increased or decreased according to blood sugar estimations. The regime should be continued postoperatively until she is taking food orally.

In choosing anaesthesia bear in mind that she also has angina, so cardiovascular stability is important. A unilateral spinal or light general anaesthesia based on a relaxant/nitrous oxide technique would fit the bill.

5. In these circumstances insulin would not be needed. Chlorpropamide is long acting and should be stopped for at least 48 hours pre-operatively. It is better to change to the shorter acting glibenclamide a week or so beforehand. No drugs or breakfast on the morning of operation and provided blood sugar is less than 10 mmol/l hypo-glycaemic agents can be restarted with the first postoperative meal.

Case History 3

Commentary

1. The most striking abnormality is in the chest X-ray, this shows a large gastric shadow behind the heart containing air and a fluid level; the patient has a large hiatus hernia with most of the stomach being in the chest. The ECG shows lateral subendocardial ischaemia which might be expected in an obese patient. Biochemical results are in the normal range.

2. Arterial blood gases taken in the supine position, breathing air. This generally shows normal PCO_2 with decreased PO_2 due to a com-bination of factors producing increased venous admixture. A mino-rity of obese patients have obesity-hypoventilation syndrome (Pickwickian) and have hypercapnia with somnolence, in addition to hypoxaemia.
Lung function tests. Rib cage movement is restricted and breathing is mainly diaphragmatic though the diaphragm may also be restricted by abdominal fat especially when lying down. This results in reduced Functional Residual Capacity (FRC) and Total Lung Capacity. Residual volume and closing capacity are unaltered so that closing capacity encroaches on FRC.
Urine and blood glucose (higher incidence of diabetes in obese patients).

3. 30 kg (43%). There are a variety of methods for estimating ideal weight one of the simplest is: ideal weight for male adult = (height in cm - 100 kg) and for a female (height in cm - 105 kg).

4. The general problems are: positioning and lifting the patient; it may be better to let him position himself on the table. Venous access may be difficult but it is essential for either general or regional anaesthesia. Intubation difficulties: one may need a detachable laryngoscope handle. Increased gastric residue of low pH with increased intra-abdominal pressure and risk of regurgitation. Cardiomegaly, increased work of the heart, increased O_2 consumption leading to subendocardial ischaemia. Those with hypoventilation syndrome may also have pulmonary hypertension, cor pulmonale and polycythaemia. Altered handling of drugs due to fatty infiltration of the liver and large mass of body fat with low blood flow; this will delay recovery from volatile agents. Variable absorption of IM drugs (more likely in fact to be SC), making post-operative analgesia difficult. Increased work of breathing with low FRC, making spontaneous ventilation inadvisable and incomplete reversal of neuromuscular blockade particularly dangerous. Postoperative hypoxaemia is exaggerated. Stress response to surgery will increase glucose intolerance.

5. The particular risk for this patient is posed by the hiatus hernia and high risk of pulmonary aspiration if precautions are not taken. The results of failing to take precautions are shown in Fig 6: aspiration.

6. Many of the problems above can be avoided by the use of regional anaesthesia but this can be difficult in the obese because land marks are obscured. Specially long needles may be required. Field block (iliohypogastric, ilioinguinal and genitofemoral nerves), spinal or epidural blockade would all be suitable.

    If general anaesthesia is undertaken opiate premedication should be limited because of postoperative respiratory depression after a short operation. Benzodiazepines may be better. Pre-induction antacid (20 ml of 0.3 Molar sodium citrate) should be given. Rapid sequence ('crash') induction with application of cricoid pressure until a cuffed endotracheal tube is in position, can be followed by balanced anaesthesia. Atracurium has theoretical advantages for muscle relaxation because of its relatively short action and rapid elimination. Halothane is best avoided because halothane hepatitis is commoner in the obese. Enflurane or isoflurane will be more rapidly eliminated. Minimal monitoring includes ECG and BP. The patient should be extubated on the left side and not until the relaxant is fully reversed and laryngeal reflexes returned. Postoperatively ventilation should be checked particularly carefully, the patient sat up and oxygen given for 48 hours. Early mobilisation and heparin prophylaxis are needed for prevention of thrombo-embolism.

Case History 4

Commentary

1. The PEFR and FEV_1 are both reduced and FEV_1/VC is 56% (normal 80%). This is characteristic of an obstructive picture, i.e. typical of asthma. There is an improvement after salbutamol which shows the obstruction to be at least partly reversible. Vital Capacity (VC) is also reduced but less so than the FEV_1 and indicates some restrictive defect, though the asthma is clearly the main problem.

2. The first set of gases would be remarkably bad in an asthmatic if they were truly arterial. PCO_2 above normal in an asthmatic is usually the prelude to exhaustion and respiratory failure. The likeliest explanation is that it is a venous sample, these being normal venous gases. The femoral vein lies immediately medial to the femoral artery, which is not a good site for blood gas sampling. This explanation is confirmed by the radial sample which shows normal pH and PCO_2 and a mildly reduced PO_2 consistent with the patient's age and clinical condition.

3. Her hypertension seems reasonably controlled on Moduretic. One would want an ECG to look for any signs of left ventricular strain or enlargement. Moduretic is a mixture of amiloride and hydrochlorothiazide and is potassium conserving, but urea and electrolytes should be checked.

4. The two most important factors in choosing anaesthesia for this patient are to avoid provoking her asthma and to provide good relaxation for the repair of a large abdominal hernia. Epidural anaesthesia will accomplish this and avoid the need for intubation. Judging by the number of drugs she is on there is probably a considerable emotional component and there may be advantages in general anaesthesia. A relaxant, nitrous oxide, opiate anaesthetic with intubation and volatile agent supplementation would be acceptable, but it would be important to avoid histamine releasing drugs, most notably d-tubocurare. Many anaesthetists also avoid thiopentone in asthmatics as it is said to cause mild bronchoconstriction.

5. Whether regional or general anaesthesia is chosen, good premedication is important. Standard anxiolytic and/or narcotic premedication may be given. Pethidine is frequently preferred in asthmatics because it relaxes bronchial smooth muscle. Steroid cover in the form of hydrocortisone 100 mg i.m. with premed must be given. It is also important to give salbutamol and beclamethasone inhalation with the premed or nebulised salbutamol via a face mask after premedication.

Case History 5

Commentary

1. The raised urea at the time of his admission is due to his being obstructed and it falls to within normal limits when the obstruction is relieved.

2. The ECG shows he has a pacemaker which is pacing on demand at 70/min. Note that where his own rate is greater than 70 there is no pacing spike.

3. Modern pacemakers are unaffected by diathermy. His particular pacemaker should be checked for this property. The diathermy plate should be positioned so that current does not go near the pacemaker (e.g. on the thigh). The pacemaker can be converted from demand to fixed rate by the application of a magnet, which should be available in theatre.

4. The fall in systolic pressure to 100 after the spinal is due to sympathetic blockade and is corrected by the infusion of Hartmann's solution. The fall that begins after an hour of operating could be due to blood loss, but the blood pressure is continuing to fall despite 2 units of blood and 500 ml of colloid. A likelier explanation is that large volumes of glycine from the irrigating fluid are leaking into the circulation (the 'TUR Syndrome'). It can be forced into open prostatic veins by the hydrostatic pressure of the irrigating fluid and can also leak if the capsule is ruptured. Both of these are more likely the longer the operation, and the more inexperienced the surgeon.

5. The diagnosis of fluid overload is confirmed by the investigations in recovery; dilutional hyponatraemia, pulmonary oedema and hypoxia with respiratory alkalosis. His confusion is due to a combination of water overload, hypotension and hypoxaemia.

6.   On examination the patient would be pale and peripherally cold, hypotensive with a raised JVP and possibly gallop rhythm. There would be fine crepitations over both lung fields. Fig 9 shows pulmonary oedema.

7.   To Intensive Care. Diuretic therapy and IPPV must be started.

Case History 6

Commentary

1.   Lung fields normal. Heart not enlarged. There is gas under the diaphragm.

2.   Perforated duodenal ulcer.

3.   Anaemic, with a microcytic, hypochromic picture suggestive of long standing iron deficiency anaemia. ECG essentially normal, sinus rhythm, rate 58/min.

4.   Abnormal plasma cholinesterase: suxamethonium apnoea.
      Septicaemia.
      Anaphylactoid reaction to an anaesthetic drug.
      Malignant hyperpyrexia.
      Porphyria.
      Inappropriate dose of drugs, poorly managed anaesthetic.

5.   Questions designed to distinguish between the above possibilites as well as the general question "Has anyone else in your family had a problem with anaesthesia".
      How long was the brother in ITU?
      Was he ventilated? For how long?
      Was he given any further instructions about future anaesthesia or drugs?
      Were measures taken to cool him?
      Patients are often surprisingly vague about family history and even their own past medical history. In limited time, one might end up not being able to exclude with certainty any of the three hereditary disorders mentioned above: abnormal cholinesterase, malignant hyperpyrexia and porphyria.

6.   It might therefore be prudent to avoid barbiturates (precipitate porphyria), suxamethonium (apnoea) and all the drugs which may

precipitate malignant hyperpyrexia of which the most important are suxamethonium, volatile agents especially halothane, atropine, phenothiazines, lignocaine, curare. This does not leave much choice but, diazepam, etomidate, pancuronium, opiates, nitrous oxide (probably) could be used.

In choosing the anaesthetic drugs one has to balance the risks: the probability of a full stomach and the possibility of some hereditary problem. One would take the usual precautions against aspiration (antacid, preoxygenation, cricoid pressure). The choice is then between using suxamethonium which undoubtedly gives the best intubating conditions or a nondepolarising relaxant which avoids any possibility of suxamethonium apnoea. For the inexperienced anaesthetist it may be better to use suxamethonium and test carefully for return of neuromuscular transmission with a nerve stimulator, accepting the fact that the patient might have to be ventilated postoperatively if he had abnormal plasma cholinesterase.

7.   Despite the haemoglobin of 8.7 g this is clearly an emergency and one would transfuse the patient during rather than before the operation. Time should be allowed for cross matching (1-2 hours) but there need be no more delay than that. Chronically anaemic patients are usually well compensated for their low Hb, by increased cardiac output and increased 2,3-diphosphoglycerate (DPG) which shifts the oxygen dissociation curve to the right. Both of these factors increase oxygen availability in the tissues. Although transfused blood should increase the haemoglobin level and hence oxygen carrying capacity there may be disadvantages. Too rapid transfusion may lead to circulatory overload and congestive cardiac failure. Banked blood is low in 2,3-DPG which shifts the dissociation curve to the left and impedes oxygen release at the tissues. For these reasons transfusion immediately preoperatively (other than for volume replacement) is not recommended. One should not get too carried away with arguments about 2,3-DPG because within 6-24 hours of transfusion the levels are restored to normal. The main reason for transfusing this patient intraoperatively is because at a level of 8.7 he has much less haemoglobin in reserve to cope with expected and unexpected operative losses.

Case History 7

Commentary

1.   This is a normal chest X-ray.

2.   The apnoea is due either to depression of central respiratory drive or peripheral neuromuscular failure.

Central depression might be due to:

a)   Hypocarbia. A minute volume of 8 litres per minute for a 50 kg patient is well over 100 ml per kilo which might be expected to maintain normocarbia. A low carbon dioxide tension will reduce the central respiratory drive.

b)   Opiate depression. Fentanyl 200 μg in half an hour is generous on top of pethidine 75 mg as premedication only an hour and a half before the end of the procedure at which point the pethidine is probably exerting its peak effect.

c)   Other general anaesthetic agents, thiopentone and halothane, may contribute to central depression of respiration.

Continuing neuromuscular blockade may be due to:

a)   Abnormal or low plasma cholinesterase causing prolonged paralysis with suxamethonium. The gene for abnormal cholinesterase is present in the homozygous form in approximately 1 in 3000 of the population. Such individuals take several hours to metabolise a single dose of suxamethonium.

b)   Failure to reverse the non-depolarising pancuronium blockade which might be encountered having used a high dose (more than 0.1 mg/kg) for a relatively quick procedure.

A combination of the above factors can cause apnoea. Finally breath-holding on the endotracheal tube in a light patient may confuse the issue.

3.   The clinical picture of a partially paralysed patient: twitching with uncoordinated attempts at muscle movement is quite different from the centrally depressed patient. A nerve stimulator should be used. Prolonged depolarising block (due to suxamethonium) will show diminished or absent twitch with no fade on tetanic stimulus. Non-

depolarising block will be characterised by fade on tetanic stimulation or the train of four, and post tetanic facilitation. Opiate depression will be rapidly reversed by a test dose of 0.1-0.4 mg of naloxone. The respiratory stimulant doxapram (1 mg/kg) will usually reverse opiate and other central depression, but is nonspecific and does not help in diagnosis. Arterial PCO_2 will rise 3-4 mm per minute if the patient is apnoeic. If there is confusion as to whether the CO_2 has risen beyond normal and hypercapnia is causing apnoea an arterial blood gas should be drawn.

4. Patients with abnormal plasma cholinesterase need to be ventilated until the suxamethonium has worn off. The process can be speeded by giving fresh blood or plasma which contains significant amounts of the enzyme. Residual paralysis with pancuronium may be treated with a further dose of neostigmine, but remember that this will worsen a suxamethonium block. Central depression can be reversed with naloxone or doxapram as above.

Case History 8

Commentary

1. His lower mandible is somewhat receding but undue difficulty would not necessarily be anticipated.

2. Features which lead one to expect difficulty are muscular patients with short necks ('bull neck'), receding mandible, prominent upper teeth particularly if there are irregular gaps, limited mouth opening, limited neck movement, large tongue, obesity especially with large breasts. Tumours or trauma to the upper airway are obvious causes but often difficult intubation cannot be predicted from the patient's appearance.

3. Call for help of a senior anaesthetist. At the level of Part I FCAnaes you are expected to demonstrate safe rather than heroic management. (This is of course true at all levels of experience!)

4. Always consider: a) Wake the patient and do the procedure under regional anaesthesia. b) Can the operation be done without intubation either by controlled ventilation on a mask, or by spontaneous ventilation? The former is impractical in an eye case, but anaesthesia can be maintained by spontaneous breathing through a nasopharyngeal tube. c) Use more complex techniques to achieve intubation. In this case (a) was chosen.

5.   Although atracurium is of medium duration of action (20-30 mins), in common with other non-depolarising relaxants it can only be reversed with neostigmine when there is some recovery of neuro-muscular function. A peripheral nerve stimulator will indicate this. Using the train of four, the fourth twitch disappears or reappears at 75% block and this can then be reversed with neostigmine 2.5-5 mg plus atropine 1.2-2.4 mg.

6.   Surgical emphysema in the soft tissues of the neck, a result of trauma to the pharynx.

7.   a)   Passing a flexible gum elastic bougie (blind) and railroading a tube over it.

      b)   Blind nasal intubation.

      c)   Intubating the trachea with a fibreoptic bronchoscope and sliding a tube over it.

      d)   Retrograde methods in which the cricothyroid membrane is pierced by a Touhy needle and an epidural catheter or Seldinger wire passed back through the cords to the mouth. This is then used to railroad a tube.

      e)   Cricothyroid puncture and jet ventilation.

      f)   Elective tracheostomy.

All of these techniques can be done awake with local anaesthesia or under general anaesthesia preferably with spontaneous breathing. b)- f) all require experience and should not be tried by the inexperienced solo anaesthetist. If there is doubt about the placement of the tube and cyanosis develops remember the golden rule "If in doubt - take it out" and ventilate by mask.

Case History 9

Commentary

1.   No. All biochemical tests are normal and nothing in the history, such as weight loss, tremor, anxiety, tachycardia, suggests thyro-toxicosis. Patients with large goitres are usually euthyroid.

2.   In hyperthyroidism T4 and/or T3 are raised and TSH is low due to

suppression by the circulating thyroid hormones. In hypothyroidism T4 is low (T3 not usually measured) and TSH is high.

3.   Lugol's iodine reduces the vascularity of the gland and is used to prepare the patient for surgery. The effect is only temporary and if the patient is not operated on within two weeks the gland escapes from control.

4.   The chest X-ray shows the trachea deviated to the right by the enlarged thyroid.

5.   Because of the deviated trachea a reinforced endotracheal tube should be used and a smaller size than usual may be necessary. The larynx itself should be easily visualised (the deviation being below this point) so no particular difficulty in intubation would be anticipated.

6.   The pulse and blood pressure are both rising. The most likely explanation is that the patient is light or even paralysed but awake (euphemistically called 'awareness'). only 50 mg of pethidine was used for premedication, with atropine which would contribute to tachy-cardia. The technique of IPPV with 66% nitrous oxide, relaxant and pethidine supplement cannot guarantee that 'awareness' will not occur. Although this patient is receiving enflurane, 0.4% is a very low concentration and may well be inadequate.

Hypercarbia is another possible explanation. Ventilation should be checked, but if the set gas flow (6 l/min) is being delivered to the patient who weighs 58 kg, this should be adequate.

Thyroid crisis or storm is highly unlikely as an explanation because the patient has always been euthyroid and when it does occur, which is rarely, it tends to be later in the operation or during recovery.

7.   If the right recurrent laryngeal nerve is damaged the right vocal cord will not move. If partially damaged the vocal fold moves towards the midline because the adductors are unopposed. If the nerve is severed completely the cord lies in the cadaveric (mid) position and in time the opposite cord compensates by increased adduction so that normal speech is restored.

8.   Hypocalcaemia due to damage to or removal of parathyroid tissue. Tetany may occur, this can be provoked by tapping the facial nerve (Chvostek's sign) or inflating an arm tourniquet (Trousseau's sign).

Calcium gluconate 10% up to 20 ml given by slow intravenous infusion will be needed.

Case History 10

Commentary

1. He has quite an extensive skull fracture over the right parietal area.

2. The positive Sickledex merely tells you that HbS is present. In the presence of a normal haemoglobin this is most likely to be Hb AS (trait). HBSS is always accompanied by significant anaemia. HBSC or HbSthal may be present without anaemia but these are rare.

3. Haemoglobin electrophoresis will give the definitive diagnosis, but this is not usually available out of hours. In this case a blood film should be examined for abnormal red cells and a reticulocyte count performed. The shortened red cell survival in HbSS leads to a reticulocytosis.

4. From the point of view of his head injury general anaesthesia, if it has to be given, should be designed to prevent rises in intracranial pressure and allow rapid recovery for postoperative neurological observations. This means ventilating the patient and avoiding halothane and enflurane. However, in this case a local block would be most suitable since it would not affect his cerebral state and would allow continued neurological assessment. Bier's block is contra-indicated (Sickle trait) but a brachial plexus block, axillary or supraclavicular, would be ideal.

Case History 11

Commentary

1. Sinus rhythm. Rate 75 per minute. Deep Q waves in V_{1-4}.
    ST segment elevated (Concave downwards) V_{1-3}.
    T wave invertion in I, aVL, V_{1-6}.

2. Anterior full thickness myocardial infarction. This is probably the reason for his admission to the hospital 6 weeks ago.

3. Fitness for anaesthesia has to be judged relative to the urgency of the operation. The evidence is that recent myocardial infarction pre- disposes to a second infarct in the postoperative period. There is no doubt that his operation should be delayed because the risk of reinfarction falls as time passes, and medical treatment can be given as an alternative to surgery for duodenal ulceration.

4. To assess the risk in this patient one can only look at large series of similar patients. These show that the risk of reinfarction for surgery within 3 months of an infarct is about 40% and the mortality is higher (up to 50%). Between 3 and 6 months the risk falls to 15%, and after a year it is no higher than in other patients. Hence the strong recommendation to delay surgery.

Case History 12

Commentary

1. In a portable AP chest X-ray the plate is behind the patient and the rays are shot from anterior to posterior. In a PA film the plate is in front and the rays come from behind. The main difference is that since the heart is nearer the front of the chest it casts a bigger shadow in the AP than the PA view.

2. There is hyperinflation of the left lung with collapse of the right lung and a pneumothorax on the right. The collapse of the right lung is due to the endotracheal tube being down the left main bronchus (not clearly seen in this portable film). This would not cause the pneumothorax which may have been caused during insertion of the right internal jugular catheter which can be seen in all three films. The blood gases show marked hypoxia with normal pH and PCO_2. This is compatible with a large shunt which one expects with only one lung being ventilated.

3. The next film shows the endotracheal tube has been pulled back and is now in the trachea, but there is still a pneumothorax and the right lung remains collapsed. There would be no improvement in arterial blood gases.

4. A drain must be inserted with an underwater seal to drain air from the pneumothorax and re-expand the right lung.

5. The lung has re-expanded. The chest drain can be seen in the bottom corner of the picture. ECG monitoring wires are seen across the lower chest.

Case History 13

Commentary

1. 2:1 heart block. The atrial rate is 84 per minute and the ventricular is 42. Only every second P wave is followed by a QRS complex.

2. Low cardiac output associated with this slow ventricular rate can cause dizziness, particularly if she changes from first degree heart block to second degree heart block (the rhythm shown here).

3. She should have a demand pacemaker inserted.

4. Certainly. If there is not time for the insertion of an internal pacemaker before surgery, temporary pacing with transvenous wires and an external box should be instituted.

READING AND REFERENCE BOOKS

The books listed here are a minimum selection that we would recommend as the basis for studying for the Part I FCAnaes Examination. Some you will already have, others you may wish to buy, all should be in a Departmental library.

ANAESTHETICS

Aitkenhead, A.R. and Smith, G. **Textbook of Anaesthesia**. 2nd edition 1990. Churchill Livingstone.

Atkinson, R.S., Rushman, G. and Lee, A.J. **Synopsis of Anaesthesia**. 10th edition 1987. Wright PSG.

Feldman, S., Harrop-Griffiths, W. and Hirsch, N. **Problems in Anaesthesia: analysis and management**. 1989, Heinemann.

MEDICINE

Vickers, M.D. **Medicine for Anaesthetists**. 3rd edition 1989, Blackwell.

Hutton, R. and Cooper, G. **Guidelines in Clinical Anaesthesia**. 1985, Blackwell.

PHYSICS AND CLINICAL MEASUREMENTS

Parbrook, G.D., Davis, B.D. and Parbrook, E.O. **Basic Physics and Measurement in Anaesthesia**. 3rd edition 1990, Butterworth Heinemann.

PHYSIOLOGY

Ganong, W.F. **Review of Medical Physiology**. 15th edition 1991. Lange.

PHARMACOLOGY

Laurence, D.R. and Bennet, P.N. **Clinical Pharmacology**. 6th edition 1987, Churchill Livingstone.

Vickers, M.D., Morgan, M. and Spencer, P.S.J. **Drugs in Anaesthetic Practice**. 7th edition 1991, Butterworth Heinemann.

INDEX

Only the keywords in the questions have been included in this index so as to enable questions on particular topics to be found.